HEROES OF A
TEXAS CHILDHOOD

BOOKS BY KINKY FRIEDMAN

*

HEROES OF A TEXAS CHILDHOOD

KINKY FRIEDMAN

ART BY COPPER LOVE

Drawings © 2009 by Copper Love. For more information, please visit www.copperlove.com

Published by Kismet Press. 965 Echo Hill Road, Medina, Texas 78055

Printed in the United States of America by Herring Printing Company, Kerrville, Tex. www.herringprinting.com

Book and Cover Design by Elizabeth Herring www.elizabethherring.com

Library of Congress Cataloging-in-Publication Data

Friedman, Kinky
        Heroes of a Texas Childhood./ Kinky Friedman. - 2nd Printing

p.   cm.
ISBN-13: 978-0-615-30685-8
ISBN-10: 0-615-30685-3

Fourth Printing December 2012

DEDICATION

This book is dedicated to the young people of Texas in the hope they may become better acquainted with some of the people upon whose shoulders they stand.

TABLE OF CONTENTS

ACKNOWLEDGMENTS

The author would like to thank the following: Sandy and Jon Wolfmueller, Wolfmueller's Books, Kerrville, Texas; Max Swafford, Sage Ferrero, Joe Herring, Jr., Sheryl Eddins, Cody Garrett, Liz LeMaire, Mary Jo Brandon, Cousin Nancy Parker, Steve Samet, Amanda Friedman, Kay Wicall, and Sean Wicall. The author would also like to express his gratitude to the artist whose work graces these pages, Copper Love.

AUTHOR'S INTRODUCTION

Heroes of a Texas Childhood is not a children's book but it could be. There are no sports figures in this book but there could have been. There are no stars from the world of entertainment except Willie Nelson, but that's not why he's in the book. Indeed, at this writing, of all the heroes, only Willie and Racehorse Haynes are still alive, yet the inspiration keeps flowing from all of them. That's why they are heroes.

Some heroes of mine, like my mother, seem yet too close to my heart to write about. So how did I select the heroes for this book? Like an old man patiently whittling on a stick. But I'm not that old. And besides, it's a big stick. It could possibly be used to climb a mountain.

Heroes of a Texas Childhood is a personal book, yet it is also a history book of sorts. That is as it should be. All historical writing, they say, is either autobiography or plagiarism. That this book is a little bit of both is freely acknowledged here.

Some of the heroes in this book are covered with glory, and some remain unsung even to this day. They are here because of the way they faced the failures, challenges, and tragedies of their lives. My friend Jim Hightower once told me that the best way to know somebody is to find out who that person's heroes are. It is an honor to share with you some of mine.

Ace Reid

Drawing From Experience

On a chilly, gray morning in November 1991 at a truckstop somewhere in New Jersey, I learned that Ace Reid had gone to Jesus. Only later did I learn from his wife Madge and from friends who'd known him much longer, how many times Ace had dodged the bullet in his life — beating leukemia in 1961, triumphing over abject poverty, and overcoming the almost inexorable forces that worked to keep him an unfulfilled, unknown cowpoke in Electra, Texas.

Ace Reid beat the odds many times in his life and not the least of these was what he managed to accomplish creatively and professionally. Though Ace's father and family were convinced that art was not a suitable occupation for a cowboy and though he had little formal education or training, Ace became without a doubt the most popular and best-loved cowboy cartoonist in the West. As his friend Elmer Kelton said: "Ace's name is known far and wide. Mention him to any cowboy or ranchman West of the Mississippi and you'll almost always get a smile."

Indeed, Ace could have probably conquered the lands East of the Mississippi if he'd tried. By 1983 his weekly cartoon series *Cowpokes* was appearing in well over five hundred newspapers, making him the biggest self-

syndicator in the world. By this time he also had eleven books in print and the Ace Reid Calendar had become a staple in rural and small town banks, hardware stores, groceries, and homes throughout the West. According to John Erickson, Ace's biographer, "Officials of the Vernon Company of Newton, Iowa, publishers of the Ace Reid Calendars, estimated that in twenty-six years one hundred million Ace Reid cartoons have appeared on calendars making him the most popular calendar artist in the West today."

But Ace Reid was far more than a cartoonist. He was a dreamer, a drinker, a character, a prankster, and a story-teller in the western tradition of Will Rogers, Mark Twain, and John Henry Faulk. Not only was Ace the World's Greatest Cowboy Cartoonist (he became to the rural West what cartoonist Bill Mauldin had been to World War II) he also was much sought after for speaking engagements. And Ace's voice was almost as unique as the man himself. He spoke with a warm, friendly, booming Panhandle twang that often had a timbre not dissimilar to a barbwire fence singing in a duststorm. And this was fitting, for Ace remembered well the duststorms, droughts, and depressions of his youth, and he drew upon these as surely as he drew upon the paper in front of him to inevitably triumph over a hard luck hand.

Ace's family had no electricity or indoor plumbing — only mosquitoes, rattlesnakes, hailstorms, and tornados — and as a youngster Ace sometimes had to work cattle at a temperature of twelve degrees below zero. Ace also recalled walking out of his house one day and watching a man with a gun hijack the postman and his truck as he came to deliver the mail. He learned later that the man was Clyde Barrow.

At age five, Ace was already drawing sketches of horses and other animals. In high school he turned a chicken coop into an art studio. In 1943 he dropped out of high school to join the Navy and see the world. His cartoons appeared in the ship's paper, but after the war, instead of heading for the Big Apple, as some New York correspondents on his ship had suggested, he went back home to Electra. For three years he tried earning a living in cattle and oil, drawing cowboy cartoons in his spare time. Ace and his wife, Madge, met in Electra in 1946, and three years later they eloped to Dallas, shortly after Ace had given up on oil and cattle and had begun selling cartoons to various newspapers. It took three more years of moving around selling art out of their car before they settled in Kerrville, where Ace was the first artist in a town now famed as an art colony.

Ace Reid never had a literary agent. He never had a publishing house. Yet he and Madge brought out thirteen volumes of his cartoons and sold them in countless numbers. Ace never had a public relations firm but Madge was able to book all the speaking engagements he could possibly want at $1,500 a night. How did the two of them accomplish all that? Ace's answer: "I was just too dumb to know I couldn't do it." Few people today believe that.

For a cowpoke who never finished high school, the legacy of Ace Reid's work reflects a highly-refined philosophic eye for the human (and animal) condition; he drew with intelligence and imagination and artistry and dignity the simple frustrations of the ordinary man.

His love and understanding of animals also comes across clearly in Ace's work. As the artist himself remarked: "I am the biggest rancher in the world. I have more sheep, horses, and cattle than anyone, and if you don't believe it, I'll sit down and draw 'em... I can't talk New York or Los Angeles but I can talk the ways of an animal."

Ace was a very colorful American and the people he gathered around him were by all standards an extremely mischievous, fun-loving bunch. One of his closest friends and running mates was the much-celebrated mayor of Luckenbach, Hondo Crouch. Ace and Hondo did the dinner, rodeo, and party circuits together as well as several notorious stints in Las Vegas, including one where Hondo was picked up on the strip by police at two o'clock in the morning mistaken for a hippie. "Naw," said Hondo. "I got an airplane." Madge Reid had indeed hired a private plane for Hondo but he had to take the cops to the airport before they'd believe him. What follows is Ace's own account of his adventures with Hondo when the Smithsonian Institute invited the newly formed Institute of Texas Cultures to send representatives to Washington in the early sixties:

"We had our Texas culture: Germans from Fredericksburg, we had our Mexicans from San Antone, we had our Czechoslovakians from down around Corpus, we had our Cajuns from East Texas, we had our Indians from out around El Paso.

"Well, old Hondo came by here in his old pickup, picked me up so we could catch the airplane. He had a couple of jugs of tequila and we got to nipping on that tequila. He had a pillowcase full of German sausages, all wrapped up. And he had some rattlesnake hides hanging out of the pillowcase with the rattlers still on the tail.

"We hit that airport. They'd see old Hondo with the sack of rattlesnakes walking through there, and he wiggled the neck of that sack and those rattlers would just rattle. They was leaving him alone.

"Then we got on the airplane. They made three mistakes. First, inviting Hondo, second, letting him on the airplane, and third, putting him on the front seat. Everybody had their eyes on Hondo.

"We took off and got about twenty-five thousand feet and old Hondo went to crawling down the aisle on his hands and knees. Sure 'nuff, there was an old fat lady there said: 'Hondo, what are you looking for?' He said, 'Oh, three of my little rattlesnakes got out and I can't find 'em anywhere.'

"That old lady squalled, throwed her legs up in the air, the whole front end of that airplane went to the back end and that plane turned up just like that. Went to thirty-five thousand feet and that pilot fighting those controls and he finally got it trimmed.

"And then he came back to trim old Hondo. He was giving him a very severe talking to and the old pilot grabbed him by the collar and was shaking him. And one old cowboy who was a prickly pear burner from down South Texas, he was part of Texas Cultures, he said: 'You turn that boy loose or I'm gonna throw your butt off this airplane.'

"And that old captain turned around and there was some Cajuns sitting there from the Sabine River, they'd never been higher than a pirogue boat and didn't like that airplane in the first place, one of 'em said: 'Oh please don't throw heem off, hee's the one that's driving thees theeng!'

"And old captain went in the cockpit, locked the door, and said, 'Jezuz Christ.' Then he called Dulles airfield that we was coming in and there was a crazy person aboard the airplane. He didn't say it was a crazy man or woman, said it was a crazy person.

"We landed there and American Airlines come in on the other runway, almost wingtip to wingtip. They've got those big old buses that come up to the door and take you up to the terminal. Well, they both hit the terminal at about the same time and the police was swarming. A little old lady got off of Continental ahead of old Hondo and she had her knitting in her little bag, and those police jerked that thing away, stomped hell out of it, broke her knittin' needles, and Hondo scooted through that line and was gone."

My personal experience with the mischief-loving side of Ace Reid came many years ago when the local cancer society declared a "smokeless day" in Kerrville and Ace and I, as the two most high-profile Kerrverts available, were tapped to be smoke-persons for the event. We were both to be monitored for twenty-four hours, twelve of which were to be spent autographing our various books and paraphernalia together in the local mall. And during this entire time neither of us was to take so much as a puff of tobacco.

For me the experience was a difficult and tedious one since I've smoked about twelve cigars a day for the past thirty years. I wasn't sure I could do it and probably wouldn't have if Ace hadn't encouraged and cajoled me and told me, "We'll be in this thing together." I also wasn't sure what unpleasant effects it might have upon the architecture of my personality.

I made it through the night without smoking but things began to degenerate that morning when we got to the mall. "We can do it," Ace told me. We signed books and calendars and shook hands with people all day and we didn't smoke. I had headaches, shaky hands, and when I finally said goodbye to Ace, I thought I saw some green spermatozoa swimming around on top of his cowboy hat. Ace himself was steady, even cheerful, during the whole course of the nightmare.

When I got back to the ranch, the first three things I did was light a cigar, pour a shot of Jack Daniel's, and call Ace. He wasn't home but Madge answered and I told her that we'd both made it through the smokeless day and to give my congratulations to Ace.

"What for?" she said. "He's never smoked a day in his life."

There are many ways to remember Ace Reid. Because of the prodigious body of his work, Ace's calendars will decorate the walls of the West well into the next century and perpetuate his humor, his wisdom, and his name. But there is something deeper in the man and his legacy to us. As his friend Tumbleweed Smith once put it: "I think Ace Reid is the soul of Texas."

Lottie Cotton

Lottie's Love

When Lottie Cotton was born, on September 6, 1902, in the tiny southeast Texas town of Liberty, there were no airplanes in the sky. There were no SUVs, no superhighways, no cell phones, no televisions. When Lottie was laid to rest in Houston, there was a black Jesus looking after her from the wall of the funeral chapel. Many biblical scholars agree today that Jesus, being of North African descent, very likely may have been black. But Lottie was always spiritually color-blind; her Jesus was the color of love. She spent her entire life looking after others. One of them, I'm privileged to say, was me.

Lottie was not a maid. She was not a nanny. She did not live with us. We were not rich rug rats raised in River Oaks. We lived in a middle-class neighborhood of Houston. My mother was one of the first speech therapists hired by the Houston Independent School District; my father traveled throughout the Southwest doing community-relations work. Lottie helped cook and baby-sit during the day and soon became part of our family.

I was old enough to realize yet young enough to know that I was in the presence of a special person. Laura Bush, my occasional pen pal, had this to say about Lottie in a letter, and I don't think she'd mind my sharing it with you: "Only special ladies earn the title of 'second mother.' She must have been a remarkable person, and I know you miss her."

There are not many people like Lottie left in this world. Few of us, indeed, have the time and the love to spend our days and nights looking after others. Most of us take our responsibilities to our own families seriously. Many of us work hard at our jobs. Some of us even do unto others as we would have them do unto us. But how many would freely, willingly, lovingly roam the cottonfields of the heart with two young boys and a young girl, a cocker spaniel named Rex, and a white mouse named Archimedes?

One way or another for almost fifty-five years, wherever I traveled in the world, Lottie and I managed to stay in touch. I now calculate that when Lottie sent me birthday cards in Borneo when I was in the Peace Corps, she was in her mid-sixties, an age that I myself am now rapidly, if disbelievingly, approaching. She also remained in touch with my brother, Roger, who lives in Maryland, and my sister, Marcie, who lives in Vietnam. To live a hundred years on this troubled planet is a rare feat, but to maintain contact with your "children" for all that length of time, and for them to have become your dear friends in later years, is rarer still.

For Lottie did not survive one century in merely the clinical sense. She was as sharp as a tack until the end of her days. At the ripe young age of ninety-nine, she could sit at the kitchen table and discuss politics or religion — or stuffed animals. Lottie left behind an entire menagerie of teddy bears and other stuffed animals, each of them with a name and personality all its own. She also left behind two live animals, dogs named Minnie and Little Dog, who had followed her and protected her everywhere she went. Minnie

is a little dog named for my mother, and Little Dog, as might be expected, is a big dog.

Lottie is survived by her daughter, Ada Beverly, the two of them have referred to each other as "Mama" for at least the past thirty years, and one grandson, Jeffery. She's also survived by Roger, Marcie, and me, who live scattered about a modern-day world, a world that has gained so much in technology yet seems to have lost those sacred recipes for popcorn balls and chocolate-chip cookies. "She was a seasoned saint," a young preacher who had never met her said at her funeral. But was it too late, I wondered, to bless the hands that prepared the food? And there were so many other talents in Lottie's gentle hands, not the least of which was the skill to be a true mender of the human spirit.

I don't know what else you can say about someone who has been in your life forever, someone who was always there for you, even when "there" was far away. Lottie was my mother's friend, she was my friend, and now she has a friend in Jesus. She always had a friend in Jesus, come to think of it. The foundation of her faith was as strong as the foundation for the railroad tracks she helped lay as a young girl in Liberty. Lottie, you've outlived your very bones, darling. Yours is not the narrow immortality craved by the authors, actors, and artists of this world. Yours is the immortality of a precious passenger on the train to glory, which has taken you from the cross ties on the railroad to the stars in the sky.

By day and by night, each in their turn, the sun and the moon gaze through the window, now and again reflecting upon the gold and silver pathways of childhood. The pathways are still there, but we cannot see them with our eyes, nor shall we ever again tread lightly upon them with our feet. Yet as children, we never suspect we might someday lose our way. We think we have all the time in the world.

I am still here, Lottie. And Ada gave me two of the teddy bears that I sent you long ago. As I write these words, those bears sit on the windowsill looking after me. Some might say they are only stuffed animals. But, Lottie, you and I know what's really inside them. It's the stuff of dreams.

Willie Nelson
Notes on a Bus

It's a Bloody Mary morning, 4:45 a.m. I'm loitering in the parking lot of a convenience store on the outskirts of Tedious, Texas, watching a large male projectile vomiting on the only pay phone in the place. Not an auspicious beginning. The mission: To travel across America on the bus with Willie Nelson.

By dawn's early light, I'm aboard Willie's beautiful touring bus, the only other two occupants being Willie's driver, Gates "Gator" Moore, and Ben Dorsey, who at sixty-five is said to be the world's oldest roadie, having worked for every major country star in the firmament, including a long stint as John Wayne's valet. I mention that being Willie's valet must be easier since the only accoutrements he employs are a pair of tennis shoes and a bandanna that has been carbon-dated and found to be slightly older than the shroud of Turin. Dorsey does not respond. The bus lurches onto the highway.

We stop to pick up Willie's sister, Bobbie Nelson, keyboard player for the band. She is a charming and gracious lady, and she likes men who smoke cigars on buses. Bobbie has known Willie longer than anyone on the planet. "He was my little brother," she says. "Now he's my big brother."

I think about my own relationship with Willie. He and I have been friends for a long time, and one of the secrets of our enduring friendship is that we've usually stayed the hell away from each other. I do not want to trick the prey, but I do want to catch him. The situation is somewhat uncomfortable and reminds me of Oscar Wilde's description of a foxhunt: "The unspeakable in pursuit of the inedible."

We pick up the man who was once Bobbie Nelson's little brother in Abbott, Texas, the place where he was born and now lives with his new love, Annie, their two infant children and their two Mexican nannies, whose only word of English appears to be *Weeeellie!* I do not bring up Willie's problems with the IRS, but Willie does. It seems Willie owes the IRS millions. Sister Bobbie is very concerned. "I don't know what people with minds of machinery will do," she says. "Willie's worked so long and hard for this, and now he could lose everything."

Willie himself does not say much about this possibility. The case is current, and he's countersuing. There is a lot of money involved. Willie plays over two hundred dates a year and earns roughly $50,000 per gig.

As the bus roars toward Texarkana on the way to Detroit, we talk about the situation. Willie, relaxed and philosophical, is not the kind of man who would be likely to jump out the window of his bus.

"You're a gypsy, Willie," I say. "And a gypsy's definition of a millionaire is not a man who has a million dollars, but a man who's spent a million dollars."

Willie laughs as we sit at the little table on the bus. His eyes look into me with all the even-mindedness of a mahatma. "It's like this," Willie says. "I have the ability to make money. I have the ability to owe money. I have

the ability to spend money. And I'm proud of it. I'm the perfect American."

*   *   *

The bus moves like a patient brush stroke across the sepia Arkansas twilight. Inside, as peaceful as a still-life painting, Willie sits across the little table, the conversation moving into the murky casino of world politics. Around midnight a storm comes up, and we see lightning lashing the Nashville skyline almost as if God is smiting the Philistines, who never understood Willie Nelson. In the song "Me and Paul," Willie acknowledges that "Nashville was the roughest," but tonight he seems to hold little rancor for the town that once drove him to lie down in the middle of snowy Broadway and wait for a truck to run him over.

"As they go," I say, "that was a fairly gutsy suicide attempt."

"At three o'clock in the morning in Nashville," says Willie, "there's not that much traffic."

As we roar through Music City, its bright lights and dark shadows do not appear to evoke any bitter memories in Willie. Ben Dorsey, the world's oldest roadie, has joined in the conversation, which has now turned to bandannas, John Wayne and the Trilateral Commission. Willie is a believer in bandannas and the Trilateral Commission, but he isn't sure about John Wayne.

"I'm a Gene Autry/Roy Rogers guy," Willie says. "John Wayne couldn't sing, and his horse was never smart."

This kind of loose talk irks Dorsey, who, of course, was the Duke's valet for many years before he worked for Willie. Dorsey staunchly defends

Wayne and relates a few narratives about beautiful women, freight elevators, seven-passenger roadsters and Tijuana, at the end of which Willie concedes to Dorsey that Wayne was indeed a great American. I inquire if it's true, as Nashville's famous Captain Midnite asserts, that Willie stole the idea of wearing the bandanna from Midnite and John Wayne. Willie contends that the bandannas and tennis shoes are not an affectation — they are the outfit he wore as a child, predating Wayne or Midnite's use of the bandanna. Dorsey takes out a John Wayne book and authenticates that the Duke wore a bandanna in a movie in 1928, five years before Willie was born.

"Do you ever think of becoming old?" I ask.

"I was old before it was fashionable." W llie says.

We stop at a truck stop on the other side of Nashville to pick up guitar genius Grady Martin. Everyone gets off the bus to eat except Willie, who usually stays on, subsisting almost entirely on fried-egg sandwiches to go and bee pollen. In the early hours of the morning, during the long haul to Detroit, Willie speaks forth on one of his favorite causes: the American farmer.

"Russia's giving its land back to its farmers," Willie says, "and here we're taking it away." The Russians, apparently, have asked Willie to speak to the Russian farmers about trusting their government, something the Russian people haven't given serious thought to in over seventy years. "I don't know how I can tell the Russians to trust their government," he says, "when I don't even trust my own."

*   *   *

When I wake up it is morning, and we're in Detroit. Everyone's already checked into the hotel except Willie and myself. I pour some coffee and peek around the curtains to find that the bus is parked right next to a green lawn with a canopy and many nice, respectable-looking suburban couples having brunch. Willie pulls the curtain back ever so slightly and peers out at the scene like a storybook princess in a tower. He can never be one of these people, and I realize his gypsy lifestyle, his incredible celebrity, and his standard wardrobe, all mitigate against it. But if he's a prisoner, I figure, I may as well interrogate.

"How many songs have you written?" I ask him.

"About a thousand," Willie says.

"How many kids do you have?

"About a thousand."

"How many wives have you had?"

"Four."

"How many albums have you made?"

"Over a hundred."

"How many cars have you wrecked?"

"Over a hundred."

"Ever been really brokenhearted?"

"I've had a trail of broken hearts," he says. "At the Hank Williams level."

*   *   *

The show at the Michigan State Fair that night is so vibrant, spirited and full of energy one might not believe every member in the seven-piece band, except Mickey Raphael and Bee Spears, is over fifty. The large crowd, seemingly as diverse as America itself, is warm and enthusiastic toward Willie — almost as if he were a personal friend. There are surprisingly large numbers of blind people, adults and children in wheelchairs, and one ambulance with the back doors open and a frail old lady lying inside. The next day I'm in the hotel bar with Larry Trader, Willie's old pal and promoter and the man who once helped my former band the Texas Jewboys escape a redneck lynch mob in Nacogdoches, Texas. I mention to Trader about the wheelchairs, the blind people, the lady in the ambulance.

"I ain't sayin' he's a doctor," Trader says. "I'm sayin' he's a healer through music."

*　　*　　*

On the large patio of a Vermont luxury hotel with a vaguely mental-hospital ambience, Jody Payne, Willie's guitar player, is telling me how he first met Willie. It was 1962, and Willie had sat in for a few songs at the West Fort Tavern in Detroit, where Payne was working. Willie sang "Half a Man," and the brilliance of the song completely blew Payne away. Then the owner of the bar came over to Payne and said: "Don't let him sing anymore. He's the worst singer I've ever heard in my life."

Willie was playing bass for Ray Price at the time. "It took Ray almost six months to realize Willie couldn't play bass," says Payne. "It took us about five minutes."

*   *   *

After the show at the Champlain Valley Fair in Vermont, the bus appears to be surrounded by farmers, Hell's Angels, and American Indians. Willie is taking a break before going out to sign autographs when he suddenly realizes that he is sitting at the table with his longtime manager Mark Rothbaum and Mickey Raphael. Seizing the creative opportunities of the moment, Willie works out a spontaneous improvisation on his song "Why Do I Have To Choose?" He opens his palms in a somewhat Christ-like manner toward Rothbaum and Raphael. Willie sings: "Why Do I Have Two Jews?"

When Willie goes outside again to meet his fans, I take the chance to wander around the backstage area at the fairgrounds. L.G., a Hell's Angel in good standing, is coordinating events with various members of the crew. Gator is organizing routes with the drivers of the three other buses in the entourage, one of which belongs to Shelby Lynne, a young female singer who's opening for Willie and who has one of the most undecaffeinated voices I've ever heard this side of Janis Joplin. Poodie, who first met Willie on the gangplank of Noah's ark, is overseeing the removal of tons of equipment from the stage. Willie's family is packing up to go back on the road. They're a ragged, eccentric, efficient crew, who look for all the world like a band of gypsies who've broken into a Rolex distributorship.

As the fairgrounds empty, I am left with afterimages. Walking far into the crowd as Willie sang "Georgia On My Mind," evoking the spirits of Hoagy Carmichael and Richard Manuel. Every person in the back of the huge fairgrounds seemingly listening to every word and every note. "Angel Flying Too Close To The Ground." The metal spokes of the wheelchairs. The pulsating neon spokes of the giant Ferris wheel in the nearby field, a world away. Childhood is close by, but you can't quite touch it. "Blue Eyes Cryin' In The Rain." Sister Bobbie playing "Down Yonder" in a style that seems to flutter bravely like a balloon, escaping to some beautiful place between a little country church and an old New Orleans brothel. "Just another scene from the world of broken dreams / The night life ain't no good life / but it's my life."

I recall walking along the back of the fairgrounds listening to Willie sing, standing in the throng, thinking the thoughts of a lifetime. "You Were Always On My Mind." Willie's voice is not what is traditionally considered a good voice, but it is a great voice and one that is capable of making you cry and comforting you at the same time. I feel a palpable sense of history passing, ephemeral as the dopplered voices on a midway ride, and yet, I know something will stay.

Earlier, backstage, Willie looked out at the crowd. "That's where the real show is," he said. "Ninety-nine percent of those people are not with their true first choice." Willie smiled. Then he added, almost to himself: "That's why they play the jukebox."

As we slowly pull out of the fairgrounds, the curtain is open a bit, and Willie is looking out the window of the bus. There appears in the crowd the face of a young girl who suddenly sees him. Her countenance reflects first disbelief, then a sort of gentle reverence, then the absolute innocence of wonder. Bobbie Nelson's little brother smiles at the girl. The scenery changes. I get back to my notebook, and I realize that there are some things Willie Nelson has that the IRS can never take away.

Tom Friedman
The Navigator

Because I'm the oldest living Jew in Texas who doesn't own real estate, and given my status in general as a colorful character, there are those who profess to be surprised that I ever, indeed, had a father or a mother. I assure you, I had both.

For many years my parents owned and directed Echo Hill Ranch, a summer camp near Kerrville where I grew up, or maybe just got older. I remember my dad, Tom Friedman, talking to all of the campers on Father's Day in the dining hall after lunch. Each summer he'd say essentially the same words: "For those of you who are lucky enough to have a father, now is the time to remember him and let him know that you love him. Write a letter home today." Many years have passed since I last heard Tom's message to the campers, but love, I suppose, has no "sell by" date.

When my father was a young boy growing up in the Chicago of the late twenties, his first job was working for a Polish peddler. The man had a horse and cart that was loaded up with fruits and vegetables, and Tom sat on the very top. Through the streets and alleys of the old West Side they'd go, with the peddler crying his wares in at least five languages and my father running the purchases up to the housewives who lived on the top

floors of the tenement buildings. There were trolley cars then and colorful clotheslines strung across the sooty alleys like medieval banners. My father still remembers the word the peddler seemed to cry out more than any other. The word was *kartofel* It is Polish for "potato."

In November 1944 my mother, Minnie, gave birth to me in a manger somewhere on the south side of Chicago. (I lived there one year, couldn't find work, and moved to Texas, where I haven't worked since.) And all this time my father was far away fighting for his country and his wife and a baby boy he might never see. Tom was a navigator in World War II, flying a heavy bomber for the Eighth Air Force, the old B-24, also known as the Liberator, which, in time, it was. Tom's plane was called the *I've Had It*. He flew thirty-five successful missions over Germany, the last occurring on November 9, 1944, two days after he'd learned that he was a brand-new father. As the navigator, the responsibility fell to him to bring the ten-man crew back safely. In retrospect, it's not terribly surprising that fate and the powers that be had selected Tom to be the navigator. He was the only one aboard the *I've Had It* who possessed a college degree. He was also the oldest man on the plane. He was twenty-three years old.

After each successful mission it was the custom to paint a small bomb on the side of the plane; in the rare instance of shooting down an enemy plane, a swastika was painted. When one incoming crew, however, accidentally hit a British runway maintenance worker, a small teacup was painted on the side of the plane, practically engendering an international incident.

Tom was a hero in what he still refers to as "the last good war." For his efforts, he received the Distinguished Flying Cross and the Air Medal with three Oak Leaf clusters and the heartfelt gratitude of his crew. Yet the commanding officer's first words to Tom and his young compatriots had not been wrong. The CO had told them to look at the man on their left and to look at the man on their right. "When you return," he'd said, "they will not be here." This dire prophecy proved to be almost correct. The Mighty Eighth suffered a grievous attrition rate during the height of the war.

After the war Tom and Min settled in Houston, where Tom pioneered community action programs and Min became one of the first speech therapists in the Houston public schools. In the late fifties they moved to Austin, where Tom was a professor of educational psychology at the University of Texas. It was in 1953, however, that my parents made possibly their greatest contribution to children far and wide by opening Echo Hill Ranch. My mother passed away in 1985, but Tom, known as Uncle Tom to the kids, still runs the camp.

Like most true war heroes, Tom rarely talks about the war. My sister, Marcie, once saw Tom sitting alone in a darkened room and asked, "Is everything all right, Father?" To this Tom replied, "The last time everything was all right was August 14, 1945." That was the day Japan surrendered.

On a recent trip to O'Hare Airport in Chicago, I commandeered a limo and drove through the area where Tom had grown up. There were slums and suburbs and Starbucks, but the trolley cars and the clotheslines and the peddler with his horse and cart were gone. "*Kartofel*," I said to the limo driver, but he just looked straight ahead. Either he wasn't Polish or he didn't want any potatoes.

Today Tom lives in Austin with his new wife, Edythe Kruger, and his two dogs, Sam and Perky. He has three children and three grandchildren. He eats lunch at the Frisco and still plays tennis with his old pals. He did not, as he contends, teach me everything I know. Only almost everything. He taught me tennis. He taught me chess. He taught me how to belch. He taught me to always stand up for the underdog. He taught me the importance of treating children like adults and adults like children. He is a significant American because by his example, his spirit, and his unseen hand, he has guided children of all ages safely through the winding, often torturous courses of their lives. One of them was me.

Tom's war is long over. Indeed, the whole era seems gone like the crews who never came home, lost forever among the saltshaker stars. And yet, when the future may look its darkest, there sometimes occurs an oddly comforting moment when, with awkward grace, the shadow of a silver plane flies inexplicably close to my heart. One more mission for the navigator.

Molly Ivins
The Conscience of Texas Politics

Molly remains living proof that you can be firmly on the left, speak the truth, and still be funny as hell. At the time of her death, on January 31, 2007, her books were all bestsellers, she was syndicated in more than four hundred newspapers, and her voice remained that of a Texas Cassandra, if you will, warning the world that we have to do better or we will all suffer the consequences of our spiritual and political complacency.

Of the cancer that killed her, she had this to say: "First, they mutilate you, then they poison you, then they burn you. I have been on blind dates better than that."

Regarding the first President Bush's efforts to play the Texan, she wrote: "Real Texans do not use summer as a verb." Regarding his son, "If you think his daddy had trouble with 'the vision thing,' wait'll you meet this one." She is also credited with having coined the nickname "Shrub" for George W. Bush. Indeed, Molly once described him thusly: "There was the president at his press conference looking just like a turtle on a fence post."

Molly Ivins was a big, brazen cowgirl who once walked into a party and said, "That boy's jeans are on so tight, if he farted he'd blow his boots off." After Pat Buchanan's speech at the 1992 Republican convention, she wrote: "It was good, but I liked it better in the original German." And Molly once described Dallas as "the town that roots for Goliath to beat David."

Though she was, indubitably, the sparkling and irreverent voice of the American left, and a three-time Pulitzer Prize finalist, she always claimed that her two greatest honors were that the Minneapolis police force named its mascot pig after her, and that she was once banned from the campus of Texas A&M.

In 1976 she began writing for the *New York Times*, whose lifeless, staid, not to say stultifyingly dull style proved tedious for the unsinkable Molly during six years of "being miserable for five times the salary." The newspaper made it a practise of heavily editing her work. In one story, Molly described someone as "having a beer gut that belongs in the Smithsonian." The *Times* edited that to read, "a man with a protuberant abdomen." Her colorful style continually clashed with her constipated, humorless editors' expectations, so, in 1982, they let her go after she wrote about a "community chicken-killing festival," describing it as a "gang-pluck."

Yet journalism was a big part of Molly and Molly was a big part of journalism. The press' sins of omission, she felt, were far worse than their sins of commission. In 1990 she wrote, "It is the stories we don't get, the ones we miss, pass over, fail to recognize, don't pick up on, that will send us to hell."

My dad, Tom, was a World War II hero, and Molly had long been one of his heroes, though he had never met her. He once remarked that Molly was the conscience of Texas politics. After Tom had a heart attack, Molly simply appeared at our doorstep in Austin one afternoon just to visit with him.

Molly lifted Tom's spirits tremendously and her gesture touched him deeply, as it did his son.

When I announced to run for governor of Texas in 2005, Molly asked me why I wanted to be governor. I answered, "Why the hell not?" Molly said, "That's perfect, that's beautiful. That's your campaign slogan." And, indeed, it was. Ever since then, if there's something I want to do in life but I'm not quite sure if I should, I remember Molly's suggestion and I ask myself, "Why the hell not!"

Molly was a truth-seeking missile. She was a devil and an angel and a spiritual chop-buster who went after anybody who got in the way of a better world. Quite often, she towered above the people she wrote about. They, as likely as not, were politicians or lobbyists; she was a dreamer, a little girl lost at the county fair who grew up somehow to be a brave, bawdy, brilliant, unabashed champion of the truth.

In an age in which the five major religions are McDonald's, Wal-Mart, Bank of America, Kentucky Fried Chicken, and Starbucks, Molly was an atheist. The *New York Times* described Molly after her death as a "liberal newspaper columnist." The *L. A. Times* obituary said she was a "political humorist and best-selling author." They were right, of course, but those are merely the words we use when we don't know what to say.

What should be said is that Molly was a voice in the American wilderness. Molly was a troublemaker and it's the sacred duty of the troublemaker to stir the putrid pot of humanity every so often to make people see that there's something more important than political correctness and that is the moral correctness to challenge the promises and prayers of the brokenhearted land she loved. She did it mostly with wit and humor, the kind of humor that sailed dangerously close to the truth without sinking the ship. There are two kinds of sailors, they say: the sailor who fights the sea and the sailor who loves the sea. Molly loved the sea.

Today she stands as a lighthouse, in this homogenized, sanitized, trivialized world, to all those who would seek the truth. Peace be with you, Molly.

Barbara Jordan
Common Humanity

It was a sweltering night in New York in the summer of 1976 as Barbara Jordan waited to climb the steps to the podium at the Democratic National Convention in Madison Square Garden. In a lifetime of firsts – the first African American woman to be elected to the Texas Senate, in 1966; the first African American to be elected president pro tempore of the senate in 1972; the first African American woman from the South to win a seat in the U. S. House of Representatives in 1972 – tonight she would achieve two more firsts. She would become the first black woman to deliver a keynote address to a national convention. It would also be the first time Barbara Jordan would be seen in public walking with a cane. Multiple sclerosis was the secret she took to her grave; she did not want to be seen as a victim.

Robert Strauss, chairman of the DNC, was standing below the stage with Barbara, watching former astronaut Senator John Glenn give the first keynote address. It was a nightmare. Glenn was droning on and on and absolutely nobody seemed to be listening. People were milling around, talking, doing interviews, leaving most of the seats empty, and all of this was on national television. Strauss was panicked.

Not helping his mood was the fact that Barbara had shown him a

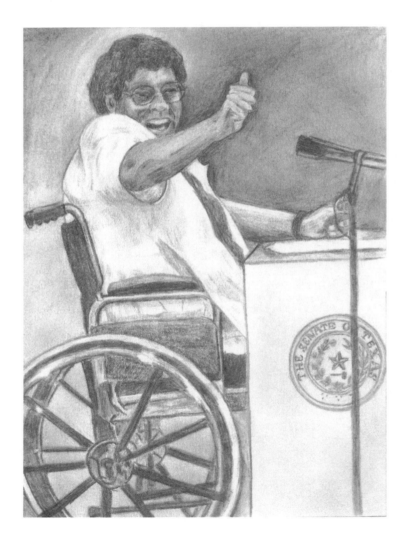

portion of the second keynote speech, which she was moments away from giving. Strauss had not been impressed. He'd only seen it the night before along with Barbara's friend, Stan McClelland, and both were unimpressed but knew it was too late to make major changes. The part that especially worried Strauss and McClelland was Barbara saying that the Democrats met for the first time in convention one hundred and some odd years ago and that what was different, what was special about tonight was that "I, Barbara Jordan, am a keynote speaker." Both men felt that many people might take that wrong, as presumptuous or even arrogant.

Mere moments before Barbara was to ascend to the podium, Strauss gave her his version of a pep talk. "Barbara," he said, "as you know there has been some criticism of my selecting you. People wanted an established national figure. Several governors were unhappy. Barbara, every chip I have is on you. Every Democratic Party chip is on you. Don't let Glenn's experience disturb you. I don't think you can quiet the crowd, and if you can't, just ignore the bastards. Speak into the camera. Remember the television audience. But if you *can* get them quieted down, then speak into the crowd."

Barbara gave Strauss a glare of disdain that traveled through his eyeballs all the way to the back of his head. It was a look, he later said, he would never forget for the rest of his life. Then she said, "Bob, if *you* can get me up the damn steps, *I* can make the damn *speech*."

And make it she did. The crowd stopped milling around and listened attentively. "It was one hundred and forty-four years ago," she began, "that members of the Democratic Party first met in convention to select their presidential candidate. Since that time, Democrats have continued to convene once every four years to draft a party platform and nominate a presidential candidate. Our meeting this week is a continuation of that tradition.

"But there is something different. There is something special about tonight. What is different? What is special?

"I, Barbara Jordan, am a keynote speaker."

The crowd rose as one sentient tower of humanity with tears in its eyes to give Barbara a five-minute standing ovation. This amazing reaction would occur twenty times within the next twenty minutes. Then it was time to go and Barbara wrapped up thusly:

"I am going to conclude my speech by quoting a Republican president and ask you to relate the words of Abraham Lincoln, relate them to the concept of a national community in which every last one of us participates: 'As I would not be a slave, so I would not be a master.'" When she had finished, absolute pandemonium broke out and the band played "The Eyes of Texas."

It was not surprising that Barbara's keynote address was such a hit; she was not only a great orator, but she spoke with a moral clarity that gave millions who heard her faith in democracy, the rule of law, and themselves. She was a patriot and a pragmatist who saw her role in civil rights not as a marcher, but as a key player working within the system.

In the Texas Senate as well as the U.S. Congress, Barbara's approach was always to engage the supposed enemy and bring out from within what she termed "the common humanity." This did not always endear her to purists, liberals, or the Black Congressional Caucus, but it was a strategy that proved remarkably effective. An example was when the Voting Rights Act, of seminal import to minorities everywhere, was in danger of expiring in 1975. To the consternation of the liberals and the Black Caucus, Barbara waltzed across to the former klansman Senator Robert Byrd, turned on some charm, and the next thing anybody knew the young Congresswoman from Texas had more than forty senators in her pocket. Largely thanks to Barbara, the bill passed.

But things weren't always that easy for Barbara Jordan. She grew up as a daughter of the old Fifth Ward, one of the poorest black areas in Houston. When she was five years old her grandfather, who owned a junkyard, gave her some sage advice that served her well, no doubt, in her future political life. "Love humanity," said her grandpa, "but don't trust 'em." That, he claimed, was the true message of Jesus.

In spite of all her successes, and they were many – or possibly because of them – Barbara Jordan, as much as any political presence of her time, was quite often the victim of personal attack. Whenever this occurred, no matter how much it hurt her inside, Barbara would never openly acknowledge the pain. It was also her firmly-held code never to counterattack personally even when she herself had been attacked in such a manner. Instead, Barbara always relegated the person to her "forgive and remember list."

Barbara Jordan's seemingly meteoric rise to the status of an American hero was in reality a hard-fought, persistent, never-give-up, personal battle against all odds. After graduating from Boston University Law School in 1959, she returned home to Houston and soon found herself campaigning zealously for JFK. Smitten by politics, she soon set her eye on becoming a candidate herself. Because she was Barbara Jordan, however, there would be many obstacles in her path in the early sixties. Indeed, a professor from Rice University once advised her that she should stay out of politics. "You've got too much going against you," he said. "You're black, you're a woman, and you're large. People don't really like that image."

Fortunately, Barbara ignored his advice. For the next three and a half decades, until her death in 1996, she continued to lead, teach, and inspire not only Texans but people all around the world. With the Constitution as her secular bible, she was an unabashed champion for anyone or any group, which she felt, had been disenfranchised from the American Dream. *E Pluribus Unum* (from many – one) was her life's dream. She worked within the system to make the words on the Statue of Liberty a reality in the lives of all the people. When she died, in fact, one of her many eulogizers called her "a monument to liberty."

In death as in life Barbara Jordan was first. She was the first African American to be buried in the State Cemetery in Austin. Only a few feet away is the grave of Stephen F. Austin. On one side of Barbara's grave is the grave of a Confederate war hero; on the other side lies the daughter of a defender of the Alamo.

"Now we must look to the future," Barbara Jordan said more than three decades ago. "Let us heed the voice of the people and recognize their common sense. If we do not, we not only blaspheme our political heritage, we ignore the common ties that bind all Americans. The great danger America faces is that we will cease to be one nation and become instead a collection of interest groups – city against suburb, region against region, individual against individual, each seeking to satisfy private wants. If this happens, who then will speak for America?"

In the eyes of many, Barbara Jordan did just that. There are those who say that Sam Houston was Texas's first real statesman. Many also believe the closest thing to a modern-day statesman Texas ever had was Barbara Jordan.

She believed that if you did not respect yourself, no one else would respect you. She had a great sense of self-respect as well as a rich sense of humor. In 1993, when Bill Clinton invited her to be his special guest at his first inauguration, he asked her to give a scripture reading at the midnight prayer service. When the service was over, a seven-year-old African American boy walked up to her with a Bible and asked her to sign it. With no hesitation whatsoever, Barbara autographed the Bible for the boy.

"Why did he ask you to sign his Bible?" asked a friend after the kid had left.

"Obviously," said Barbara, "I can only conclude that he must have thought I wrote it."

Audie Murphy

To Hell and Back

On January 26, 1945, Second Lieutenant Audie Murphy woke up in the forest just outside of Holtzwihr, France to find his hair had frozen to the ground. At 3:00 a.m. he was placed in charge of Company B, as the only officer left commanding only eighteen men capable of manning the front lines. The company had once consisted of two hundred and thirty-five men.

As the frigid, foggy morning rolled relentlessly on, Audie could not have known that by the end of the day his name would forever be etched into the vaunted hall of heroes of American warfare. By any standard Audie Murphy was a hero; he was also the unlikeliest of heroes. The mere fact that he'd even gotten into the war was remarkable considering the circumstances.

The seventh of twelve children of poor sharecroppers, Audie Murphy was born on June 20, 1924 near Kingston in Hunt County, Texas. Audie spent his days picking cotton and hunting small game in the forest to help feed the large, impoverished family. Distant from the American dream, life was tough for the Murphys and it got even tougher when Audie's father ran off in 1940. The following year his mother died. The fact that Audie was so highly skilled with a rifle may have played a big part in the survival of his younger siblings because, with both parents gone, he was the only breadwinner they had.

Everything changed, however, in December of 1941 when the United States declared war on Japan and the Axis powers. He later recalled that fateful moment on December 7, 1941, when millions of young American lives were changed. "I ran into the mail carrier on the way back from squirrel hunting," he said, "and he told me about it." Audie remembered thinking two things almost simultaneously when he first heard that the Japanese had bombed Pearl Harbor. The first was, "They can't do that!" and the second was, "Where's Pearl Harbor?"

Audie rushed to enlist, his first choice being the Marines. The Marines wasted little time in turning him away. This was not terribly surprising; in 1941 Audie Murphy, not quite eighteen, was only five feet five inches tall and weighed a mere one hundred and ten pounds. His height and weight fit perfectly into the statistical average of an American girl. The recruiters did not believe he looked like the stuff of which Marines were made. It was to be their loss.

Next Audie tried to join the Army Paratroopers, but once again, he was turned away. Finally, he attempted to enlist in the Army as an infantryman. He was again rejected, but this time he was told to come back when he was old enough. He waited and his notion of what was to be his patriotic duty burned brighter.

On his eighteenth birthday Audie Murphy was finally accepted into the regular Army as an infantryman. After completing basic training at Camp Wolters, Texas, he went to advanced infantry training at Fort Meade, Maryland. Eventually, he was shipped overseas and joined B Company, 1st Battalion, 15th Infantry Regiment, 3rd Infantry Division, operating in North

Africa. Arriving early in 1943, he saw little action as North Africa was in the mopping up stage. His baptism of fire came five months later when he landed in Sicily on July 10th. Audie distinguished himself under fire and the captain promoted him to corporal.

Audie excelled once more at the Invasion of Salerno and was promoted to Sergeant. At Anzio he was offered a battlefield commission to Second Lieutenant. This, however, necessitated his leaving his unit, so he passed on the promotion. After breaking out of the Anzio beachhead, fighting their way to Rome, the 3rd Division made yet another landing on August 15, 1944, in Southern France.

Three hours after landing, Audie's battalion found itself pinned down on a ridge with German machine guns covering every avenue of approach. Audie commandeered a .30 caliber machine gun and, with only one belt of ammunition, used short bursts to make the Germans duck down. Out of ammunition, Audie and Private Lattie Tipton, charged and silenced the first enemy position. Tipton noticed a German soldier waving a white flag and, standing up to take the man prisoner, was shot by a single rifle bullet. Audie was enraged. Using a German machine gun and several grenades, he charged all the enemy positions single-handedly and killed all the German soldiers within them. For this remarkable action, he was awarded the Distinguished Service Cross.

As Audie Murphy continued to perform feats of heroism and courage beyond the call of duty, he began to become a legend in the infantry, like the famous Roger Young in the Pacific theater of the war. Bronze stars, silver stars, and purple hearts started rolling in, but nothing seemed to stop him. He was called to headquarters and discharged from the army as a sergeant, then commissioned as a second lieutenant. He returned to his platoon, but this time he was in charge.

And so it was that Audie Murphy moved from the forests of childhood to the forests of manhood. On that foggy, freezing afternoon near Holtzwihr, France, around two o'clock, six German tanks and hundreds of snowcape-clad German soldiers appeared out of the bone-chilling mist. Audie grabbed the phone to order artillery fire, but he felt pretty sure the company was doomed. One of his tank destroyers had slid into a ditch and had to be abandoned, and the opening barrage by the Germans knocked out the other one. A tree-burst killed his machine gun squad. "At that moment," he wrote, "I knew that we were lost."

The situation appeared hopeless as the German tanks moved close enough to use their machine guns. Audie ordered everybody back into the forest, planning to stay himself in order to direct artillery fire. He'd emptied his carbine and saw that the Germans were no more than fifty yards away. Taking only his telephone with him, he jumped aboard the burning tank destroyer, which was liable to blow up at any minute, and began raking the Germans with "the perfectly good machine gun" atop the blazing metal carcass.

With an estimated two hundred and fifty Germans swarming all around him, Audie kept firing the machine gun and directing artillery fire on the phone. At one point he was asked, "How close are the Krauts?" His reply: "Just hold the phone and I'll let you talk to one of the bastards." Twelve of them, indeed, trying to out-flank him, began moving single file down a ditch less than fifty yards away. Audie "stacked them up like cordwood."

When asked over the phone if he was all right, he responded, "I'm all right, Sergeant. And what are *your* postwar plans?"

Completely exposed to machine gun, machine pistol, and 88-shell fire, two times the tank destroyer took direct hits obscuring him in smoke and flames. When it was over, the remaining Germans in full retreat, the young Lieutenant stepped off the tank destroyer, his trouser leg covered with blood, and walked back to the forest. Moments later, the tank destroyer blew up.

For this daring action, Audie Murphy received the highest accolade his country could give, the Medal of Honor. In the end, the kid who was repeatedly rejected by almost every branch of the military became the most highly decorated soldier in American history. When he returned, he chronicled his exploits in a book called *To Hell and Back*, later made into a movie in which he also starred. It was a role he was born to play.

Yet, while men such as Ronald Reagan and John Wayne had spent the war in Hollywood, not so, Audie Murphy. According to Audie, he, and the men like him who never came back, "fought to buy the freedom the rest of us cherish and abuse."

Sam Rayburn
The Incorruptible One

Heroes are not always bold, brash, colorful people. Some of them are quiet, dedicated, behind-the-scenes individuals who know themselves and work within the system to get things done for the betterment of all. Such a man was Sam Rayburn.

"Mr. Sam," as he was often called, served in the U.S. House of Representatives for forty-eight years, and as Speaker of the House for seventeen years, more than twice as long as any of his predecessors. He hated railroads, banks, utility companies, the rich, the Republican Party, and Yankees in general. Indeed, as the son of a Confederate cavalryman, Sam, according to a friend, "never stopped hating the Yankees." Yet he was probably the only man in Washington who kept two pictures on his desk side-by-side – Franklin D. Roosevelt and Robert E. Lee.

One of the reasons Mr. Sam championed the farmer, the working man, and the poverty-stricken was that, no matter how powerful he became, he never forgot who he was or where he came from. Born in 1882, the eighth of eleven children, he picked cotton at the age of five on the family farm northeast of Dallas in Fannin County. It was backbreaking, lonely work. Though he never got over the loneliness, it gave him an incredibly strong spine.

Years later, as one of the most powerful and influential men in Washington, banks and railroads and lobbyists continually came to him offering various forms of bribery. When gifts or money were offered or implied, Mr. Sam always and invariably had but one response: "I am not for sale." He preferred to shape legislation by working quietly in the background instead of being in the public spotlight. He won a well-deserved reputation for integrity and fairness that was never tarnished in all his many years in Washington. It was often said, "No one can buy Sam Rayburn."

In 1912, at the age of thirty, he was elected to Congress. "I will not deny that there are men in the district better qualified than I to go to Congress," he said, "but, gentlemen, these men are not in the race." It didn't take long for the House to realize that a giant was among them. Mr. Sam was not only an expert at procedural matters; he was also an expert at understanding human beings. When he spoke of what was right or just or honorable, he meant just that. "There are no degrees in honorableness," he said. "You are or you aren't."

When Mr. Sam had been in Congress for decades and was already a legend, reporters frequently quoted the advice he'd often given to young congressmen, "To get along, go along." The reporters assumed that he himself had gone along with the party or the powers that be even if he hadn't agreed with them. This was decidedly not the case. Even as a very young congressman, he walked his own road. He was once summoned as a freshman in Congress to the White House to meet his hero, President Woodrow Wilson. The subject was whether the government should try to reign in the railroads, the president being against it, and Mr. Sam being for it. The president used

all of his considerable powers of persuasion and made it abundantly clear how vital it was for the young congressman to "go along" with him. Mr. Sam answered the man he once wrote of as his "clean and matchless" idol in one sentence. "I'm sorry I can't go along with you, Mr. President," he said. Then he left the room without another word.

Mr. Sam played a vital role in legislation impacting the lives of the people of America. He was a major architect of everything from the Federal Trade Commission, to eight-hour work days, to almost all of the New Deal legislation, plus a great many populist advances that the public remained unaware of because of his backstage modus operandi. Perhaps even more important, particularly in light of what we think of as politics today, Mr. Sam set a tone of integrity and truthfulness that permeated all his dealings in the House and trickled down to others who perhaps were not as truthful. "He knew when a man was telling the truth," one of his colleagues once said. "He was an expert at sizing up the motives of what made human beings tick." Indeed, Mr. Sam's unseen hand was probably behind more legislation than anyone knows. "Let the other fellow get the headlines," he said, "I'll take the laws."

Through his entire boyhood, Sam Rayburn's life had been the cotton fields, plowing, and not much else. "Many a time when I was a child and lived way out in the country," he observed a lifetime later, "I'd sit on the fence and wish to God that somebody would ride by on a horse or drive by on a buggy – just anybody to relieve my loneliness. Poverty tries men's souls," he said. "Loneliness breaks the heart."

Not all lonely people are great, but there is a certain linkage between loneliness and greatness and for his entire life Sam Rayburn seemed to be cursed and blessed with both.   He gave the American people, his Texas constituents, and the House of Representatives more than forty-eight years of continuous service, the longest record ever established (at the time of his death in 1961).   He was routinely courted by lobbyists for the banks, the railroads, and the utility companies and turned down everything from free railroad passes to all travel expenses, many of which he was legally entitled to.   He is widely considered by historians to be the most effective Speaker of the House in U.S. history.

The kind of quiet hero that Sam Rayburn was may never truly be appreciated by the public.   Even the New Deal legislation, of which he was often the major architect, is seldom associated with him today.   And not many of today's politicians appear to have followed in the footsteps of "The Incorruptible One."

All of this would probably not have surprised Mr. Sam.   He died with less than fifteen thousand dollars to his name and was posthumously awarded the Congressional Gold Medal.   "A jackass can kick a barn down," he once said, "but it takes a carpenter to build one."

Racehorse Haynes
God Bless You, Mr. Racehorse

Richard "Racehorse" Haynes, undeniably one of the greatest criminal defense attorneys in the world, was born in Houston in 1927 to a family so poor that at age two he had to be shipped off to San Antonio to live with his grandmother. His granny was a little over four feet tall, drank a pint of gin a day, and taught young Richard so well that he was able to fill out the forms himself at school in order to bypass the first and second grades.

Back in Houston, Haynes went to junior high where he picked up the name "Racehorse" from a disgruntled football coach. On two consecutive plays, Haynes was unable to break through the line, so he headed rapidly for the sidelines, thereby racking up fifty yards without advancing the ball. "What do you think you are?" shouted the coach. "A racehorse?"

Unlike Audie Murphy, Racehorse was successful at making an underage entry into the military during World War II. On February 19, 1945, when he was not yet seventeen years old, Racehorse Haynes was already engaged in battle, fighting with the U. S. Marines at Iwo Jima in the Pacific theater of the war. At one point, Racehorse was missing for twenty-six days but he was one of the few who lived to tell about it.

Racehorse's life is a rags to riches story yet, as so often happens, it

was the rags that made the man. In 1938, in front of a movie theater where he sometimes saw cowboy movies for a nickel, he was arrested by a juvenile officer for vandalism — writing his initials in the wet concrete. Fifty-three years later, along with Dr. Denton Cooley, Dan Rather, and other notables, he was asked to write his name again and record his footprints in cement in front of the same movie house, as part of the "Heights Walk of Honor."

He's been known to do whatever it takes, within the law, to prove his client's innocence. This includes drinking a glass of Ortho-Sevin pesticide, shocking himself repeatedly with an electric cattle prod, and, legend has it, nearly crucifying himself to a tree. Possibly the most dangerous thing he ever did, however, was in the late forties when, with a tractor-like extension, he drove a Ford convertible from Fort Worth to Houston while sitting in the back seat and steering with his feet. He did not do that to impress a jury, he says. He did it "just for the hell of it."

"I don't get people off," he says. "The jury acquits them." He contends that the guilty are sometimes in more need of the help the law can provide than are the innocent. "I've been conned a couple of times," he says. "I've spent a lot of time thinking Humpty-Dumpty was pushed. But I can't prove it."

"There's always the chance that justice will be done," says Racehorse. He seldom if ever allows his client to take the stand for himself or indeed to say anything at all to the court. Most people, he contends, are uncomfortable in the courtroom setting and so they may appear stilted or unnatural to a jury thereby jeopardizing their own case. Only once, as a younger lawyer, did he let a defendant speak for himself.

"I believed my guy was innocent and apparently the jury agreed," says Racehorse. "So when the bailiff handed the verdict to the judge and the judge declared 'Not Guilty,' I shook hands with my guy and told him he could thank the jury if he wished. So he stands up and he says to the jury, 'Thank you. I'll never do it again.'"

Racehorse once represented two Houston cops who stood accused of causing the death of a man in their custody. He moved successfully for a change of venue to New Braunfels, which, at the time, was not known for its progressive mores. After the trial, a reporter asked him, "When did you know that you'd won the case?" Racehorse answered, "When they seated the twelfth former U-boat commander in the jury box."

During the infamous "Kerrville Slave Ranch Trial," Racehorse did indeed shock himself several times with an electric cattle prod in front of hundreds of local Kerrverts one afternoon on the courthouse lawn. "It hurt," he says, "but it wasn't lethal." Racehorse's client, who allegedly helped torture a drifter to death with the device (the homemade tape recordings of the torture sessions were played at the trial) was acquitted by the jury.

Another of Racehorse's clients, T. Cullen Davis, was said to be the richest man ever to be brought up on a murder charge. Davis allegedly shot and killed his stepdaughter and shot and wounded his wife in 1976 in his six million dollar mansion on one hundred and forty-eight acres near downtown Fort Worth. Davis claimed he was in a movie theater by himself at the time of the shooting watching The Bad News Bears. After being acquitted, he went on to become an evangelical preacher.

Yet amongst all his many courtroom victories, there is one that shines the brightest. It was a trial that had taken place in the late fifties. It received almost no publicity and he'd received no fee for his work. Yet, according to Racehorse, it still remains the closest to his heart.

He was defending a black man who stood accused of theft of construction materials, a charge Racehorse felt was clearly a frame-up. When the verdict of "Not Guilty" was brought in, the man, his two hundred and fifty pound wife, and a half a dozen of his children all ran to the middle of the courtroom, jumping up and down and hugging Racehorse.

That night he was invited to a little party out in the ghetto. It was a shotgun-railroad house like the kind put up by the company store. The man and his wife were there, all the kids, the old grandma. There was barbecue and soda pop. And on the walls, the kids had taken crayons and written: "God Bless You, Mr. Racehorse."

Ann Richards
A New Day for Texas

The 1990 Texas governor's race pitted Democrat Ann Richards, a divorced mother of four and recovering alcoholic, against the Republican, bilingual multi-millionaire entrepreneur and rancher Clayton Williams. The Republican Party began pouring millions into the Williams campaign once they saw one of the earliest polls by the *Houston Chronicle*. It showed Williams clobbering Richards by forty-eight percent to thirty-three percent. Very few observers, indeed, thought that Ann had a prayer.

But Williams turned out to be decidedly gaffe-prone. In March he invited the press to his ranch in West Texas. When the scheduled activities were rained out, however, he told them the following: "The weather is like rape. If it's inevitable, you might as well lie back and enjoy it."

Later in the campaign, he told of going to Mexico in his youth in order to "get serviced." He claimed that Ann was an "honorary lesbian" because of her pro-gay rights positions. He also revealed that he'd paid no income tax in 1986. The icing on the cake was when he refused, on live television, to shake Ann's extended hand, instead saying, bitterly, "I'm here today to call you a liar." The women of Texas were already upset about the rape joke, but refusing to shake hands with a lady seemed ungentlemanly to

the men as well.

Ann went on to win one of the most amazing upsets in Texas politics. Molly Ivins later commented, "If they'd only nailed Clayton Williams in a box and sent him out-of-state for eight months, he would've been the governor."

When Ann Richards was elected Governor of Texas in 1990, she was only the second female governor Texas had ever had. The first one, almost sixty years earlier, was Ma Ferguson who, regarding bi-lingual education, once famously said, "If English was good enough for Jesus Christ, it's good enough for Texas." Ann Richards was known for saying some pretty colorful things herself, but she brought a spirit, wit, and vitality to the governorship that Texas hadn't seen since, well, Ma Ferguson.

Ann grew up in Waco, attended Baylor University on a debate scholarship, and moved to Austin where she received a teaching certificate from the University of Texas. She taught social studies and history at Fulmore Junior High School in Austin but politics pulled her away. She campaigned for such progressive and liberal candidates as Henry B. Gonzalez, Ralph Yarborough, and future U. S. District Judge Sarah T. Hughes. She worked to elect such liberal Democrats to the legislature as Sarah Weddington and Wilhelmina Delco. She also presented training sessions and workshops all over the state to teach campaign techniques to women candidates and campaign workers.

After winning the Democratic primary in 1982 for state treasurer, Ann beat her Republican opponent that year to become the first woman to win a statewide office in Texas in more than fifty years. In 1986, she was re-elected.

Richards delivered the keynote address at the Democratic National Convention in 1988 and that really put her on the map nationally. She came down hard on the Reagan Administration and Reagan's vice-president, George H. W. Bush. Her Texas charm and witty remarks won the day. "Poor George," she said. "He can't help it. He was born with a silver foot in his mouth." She also said something that is just as true today as it was back then. She said, "When we pay billions for planes that won't fly, billions for tanks that won't fire, and billions for systems that won't work, that old dog won't hunt. And you don't have to be from Waco to know that when the Pentagon makes crooks rich and doesn't make America strong, it's a bum deal."

In 1990, Ann Richards was elected governor of Texas. She reformed the state bureaucracy, saving the state six billion dollars. She also reformed the Texas prison system, increasing prison space, reducing the number of violent offenders released, and establishing substance abuse programs for the inmates. Treatment for minor offenders, not incarceration, she felt, was the answer to massive prison over-crowding in Texas.

One of the reasons Ann Richards was so effective governing what has largely become a red state, was her basic integrity and her reliance upon people like Barbara Jordan, the first black U. S. Congresswoman elected from the South. She was, for all practical and spiritual purposes, Ann Richards' mentor.

Though Ann's strong code of ethics may have been steeled and shaped by people like Barbara Jordan, her laser-like wit was all her own. Ann was that rare bird – a true feminist with a super-sized sense of humor. She was known for her big hair, big laugh, and big dreams for Texas. But she was not hesitant to mix humor with politics, something terribly lacking in today's cowardly, politically correct crowd.

During the campaign she was asked about the concealed weapons bill. Someone posed the question to her, "Wouldn't the women of Texas feel better if they could carry guns in their purses?" Ann replied, "Well, I'm not a sexist, but there is not a woman in this state who could find a gun in her handbag, much less lipstick."

One of her most famous and oft-quoted lines was regarding a cause close to her heart, women in politics. In her keynote address to the convention she observed, "Ginger Rogers did everything Fred Astaire did. She just did it backwards and in high heels."

And then there's this, on November 15, 1998, from the *Fort Worth Star Telegram*: "Kinky saved his first animal in 1979 when he rescued a cat from a shoebox in Chinatown, but he didn't get nonprofit status until spring. That came after he smooth-talked his buddy Willie Nelson and his pal, former Governor Ann Richards, into helping him form a board of directors for the Utopia Animal Rescue Ranch. Richards told Kinky, 'I hope this isn't something I'm going to regret for the rest of my life.'"

It won't be, Ann. I promise.

Sam Houston
The Magnificent Barbarian

Sam Houston was once asked which of his many titles he cherished the most – Governor of Texas, Governor of Tennessee, Congressman from Tennessee, Senator from Texas, General of the Texas Army, or President of the Republic of Texas? None of those, he responded. The title he cherished the most, he claimed, was "teacher," for, in 1812 at the age of nineteen, he built and taught in the first one-room schoolhouse in Tennessee.

Sam's answer provides us with a glimpse into the true greatness of the man they called "The Magnificent Barbarian." His spirit, indeed, probably more than any other, was to shape the early emotional history of the state that would be known as Texas. Sam was righteous without being self-righteous; fiery yet reflective and thoughtful; stubborn, independent, hell-bent, honorable, courageous, out-of-control, and visionary. After capturing Santa Anna in the follow-up to the Battle of San Jacinto, in a much-decried magnanimous gesture, he spared the bloody dictator's life. This, after Santa Anna had all prisoners put to death at Goliad and the Alamo. This action was not simply the Christian thing to do; this was Sam, figuring correctly, that the move would expedite Texas' move toward independence.

There are many who feel that Sam, not Stephen F. Austin, should be hailed as the true spiritual father of Texas. Indubitably, Sam was more of a wild child. Yet he had a destiny wrapped around him like the serapes and Indian blankets he sometimes wore, topped off with an outlandish sombrero. For destiny it was that had led him on his circuitous path to Texas, and, like a secular Moses, helped him lead the Texans to a promised land he would never see.

Like any such seminal, formative figure of the past, rumors and mystery necessarily swirl around the life of Sam Houston. Why did he suddenly leave his successful political career and his new young bride in Tennessee? What really occurred and what changes took place within him during the time he lived with the Indians? Was he a lone wolf following his own counsel or was he, as some historians suspect, an "undercover agent" working for his mentor, President Andrew Jackson, to secure Texas for the United States?

At the heart of Sam's abrupt resignation as governor of Tennessee in 1827 was most likely a matter of the heart. He had married eighteen-year-old Eliza Allen and somehow this union did not blossom into a true relationship. As a matter of personal honor, or perhaps to protect the reputation of the girl, Sam took the secrets of his honeymoon to his grave. He left Tennessee under a cloud of scandal, eschewing "civilization" to live with the Indians. The only thing history records for certain is that, eventually, Tennessee's loss was to be Texas' gain.

What transpired when Sam lived with the Cherokee is hard to know for sure since few records were kept and he was drinking heavily much of the time. His alleged drunkenness and his abandonment of his office and his wife

reportedly caused some strain in his close relationship with Andrew Jackson, but time healed the rift. Living with the Cherokee also seemed to heal Sam Houston. He married a Cherokee widow, Tiana Rogers Gentry, and set up a trading post called Wigwam Neosho near Fort Gibson, Cherokee Nation. The tribe embraced Sam to such an extent that it even conferred an Indian name upon him, *Co-lon-neh*, meaning "The Raven." Some sources also suggest the title translates to mean "Big Drunk."

However one assesses Sam's time with the Indians, it must be said that he was one of the very few white men of his day to have a loving and respectful relationship with Native Americans. The Cherokee called Sam their brother and, for his part, Sam often interceded with the government on their behalf and spoke for Native American rights to the highest office in the land, i.e. his pal, Andrew Jackson. The tragic treatment of Native Americans is a chapter of American history written in blood, though Sam Houston fought with all his heart to keep it from being so. Sam, soon to be commander-in-chief of the Texas army, negotiated a peaceful settlement with the Cherokee in February 1836.

The Alamo fell the next month and, whether Sam had been plotting with Andrew Jackson or working entirely on his own, he was the right man in the right place at the right time. On April 21, 1836, Sam led the Texas army to a resounding victory over Santa Anna at the Battle of San Jacinto. In less than eighteen minutes it was over, and Santa Anna was forced to sign the Treaty of Velasco, granting Texas its independence. From his first footsteps onto Texas soil, Sam was at the forefront of shaping the state, politically, militarily, and spiritually. Like Socrates and Jesus before him, however, he was a visionary whose light of truth would be extinguished at the hands of his own people.

In 1845, after the annexation of Texas, Sam, as senator in Washington, clearly saw the doomed direction the country was taking. He spoke out against the growing sectionalism, blaming it on the extremists of both North and South. In 1850, eight years before Abraham Lincoln, Sam Houston told the Senate, "A nation divided against itself cannot stand." He correctly predicted the Kansas-Nebraska Act of 1854 would cause a sectional rift that would ultimately lead to war. "What fields of blood, what scenes of horror," he intoned before his fellow senators, "what mighty cities in smoke and ruins. It is brother murdering brother. I see my beloved South go down in the unequal contest in a sea of blood."

Few listened in Washington and even fewer in Texas. At the age of seventy, Sam toured the state, running for governor as an independent, trying one last time to convince his fellow citizens not to secede from the union. Though he won the race, it deeply scarred Texas' greatest statesman. Newspapers called him a traitor. Ugly mobs often gathered when he showed up to speak. People threw stones at the aging war hero who had played such a pivotal role in giving them their independence. Sam's life was threatened. He never, however, lost his sense of forgiveness or his sense of humor.

"I can forget that I am called a traitor," he said.

And when asked by a reporter what he thought of another politician who'd been crisscrossing the state zealously clamouring for secession, Sam had a ready answer. "He has all the characteristics of a dog," he said, "except fidelity."

Governor Sam Houston was soon forced to resign when he refused to sign an oath to the Confederacy. He retired, brokenhearted, to his home in Huntsville where the hills reminded him of his boyhood home in Tennessee.

On July 26, 1863, with his third wife, Margaret, at his side, Sam died. His last words were, "Texas – Margaret, Texas!"

Heman Sweatt
The Trailblazer

A hero can come in any size, shape, or color; he or she can emerge at any time or any place. The one thing most heroes seem to have in common is that they do not believe that they're really heroes. I just did what anybody would have done, they often say. This, of course, is not true. That's why we call them heroes.

My dad, Tom Friedman, a hero himself, always felt that you could judge a person by the size of his enemies. If you're just bickering with your neighbor over where to put your fence line, that doesn't tell us much. But if you agree to be the human guinea pig, the moral lightning rod, the soldier that leads the way into battle with twin giants, that is something almost nobody would do. The giants, in this case, were called "Separate but Equal" and "Segregation." The hero was named Heman Sweatt.

Heman Sweatt had a very nice, comfortable, not to say complacent, life before 1945 when, as a black man in Texas, he decided to go to law school. Heman was married to his high school sweetheart, owned his own home in Houston, and was the local secretary of the National Alliance of Postal Employees. The NAACP and Thurgood Marshall were having a tough time finding plaintiffs for civil rights lawsuits in the forties. It was not surprising that no one wanted to be at the center of the firestorm; it would require enormous dedication on the part of the chosen individual and it would be almost guaranteed to throw that person's life into chaos.

The NAACP could not find a qualified candidate to be a plaintiff in a massive lawsuit they were formulating to equalize educational opportunities at the University of Texas. It was during a meeting at the Wesley Chapel in Houston that Heman stepped forward to volunteer for a gig that, for better or worse for him, would become an important piece in the mosaic of civil rights destiny. He later referred to this decision as happening in a "brash moment," but it is important to note that the moment occurred many years before people like Rosa Parks and Martin Luther King would be lighting the way.

Heman was not unprepared for the arduous journey ahead. He'd graduated from Wiley College, the only accredited black university in the state at the time, and he'd done graduate work at Michigan. At Wiley he'd been inspired by a teacher, Melvin B. Tolson, poet laureate of Liberia, who spoke out powerfully against racial discrimination. Furthermore, Heman's time was filled with preparations to get him ready to register for classes at the University of Texas. Legal funds were raised, NAACP leaders met with him constantly, and his college records were carefully evaluated.

Finally, on February 26, 1946, Heman walked into the law school at the University of Texas and attempted to register for classes. The only thing he wanted, he stated, was to occupy one seat in a law school classroom and to go on from there to practice law in Texas. UT president, T. S. Painter, and other university officials discouraged him from applying. The matter of Heman's admission was sent to Grover Sellers, the Texas Attorney General,

who, on March 16, 1946, voiced a desire to uphold "Texas' wise and long-continued policy of segregation."

Two months later, Heman filed suit in the 126th District Court of Travis County under Judge Roy Archer, but proceedings were painfully slow. The judge gave the state six months to come up with a "substantially equal" course of legal instruction. Six months later, with still no law school for African Americans, the case was sent to a lower court for trial. The state selected the basement of a building on East 13th Street in a black, low-income neighborhood. The "separate but equal" idea was clearly working against Heman, producing little more than a sham Jim Crow law school. Thus, the strategy would have to be changed. "Whether we like it or not," said Thurgood Marshall, "we are now faced with the proposition of going to the question of segregation as such."

Heman and his supporters had lost at every level of the Texas court system, but in 1949 the case finally got to the U. S. Supreme Court. In *Sweatt v. Painter*, the Court sided unanimously with Heman. This decision, in June 1950, paved the way for the building blocks of "separate but equal" and segregation itself to begin to crumble. In September of that year, Heman dutifully registered for classes at the University of Texas School of Law.

But in human affairs it seems that all progress comes with a price. Like Audie Murphy, Heman, in his way, had struggled valiantly for six years to "buy the freedom the rest of us cherish and abuse." Thurgood Marshall wrote to Heman, "If it had not been for your courage and your refusal to be swayed by others, this victory would not have been possible."

And what was the price? Heman had lost his marriage, his home, and his job. He'd been attacked, threatened, vandalized, tormented, mocked, and turned away by an evil system in its dying throes of desperation, yet he would not be denied. He was the victim of cross burnings. He was hospitalized several times for physical and emotional exhaustion. "I don't think anyone can possibly realize the wear and tear on personal emotions one suffers in going through six years of this kind of struggle," he would reflect later.

He never finished law school. He never achieved his dream of becoming a lawyer. Yet many others who followed in his footsteps were able to realize their own dreams because of the personal sacrifices he made. Blessed is the match that kindles the flame.

In 1987, a portion of the UT campus was renamed the Heman Sweatt Campus, and, at the University of Texas School of Law, a scholarship was established in his memory.

Henry B. González

In the Minority

"Why did they name Gonzales Gonzales," Henry B. Gonzalez asked rhetorically, "if the name wasn't honored in Texas at the time?" It was May of 1957 and Henry B., the first Tejano to win a seat in the Texas Senate, had been talking to a virtually empty room for almost three hours, with nineteen more to go. It would be – and still is – the record for the longest filibuster in the Texas Senate.

"Why did they honor Garza along with Burnet?" he continued. "My own forebears in Mexico bore arms against Santa Anna. There were three revolutions against Santa Anna – Texas was only one of its manifestations. Did you know that Negroes helped settle Texas? That a Negro died at the Alamo?"

Molly Ivins described that year and that legislative agenda as "one of the ugliest times in Texas history." Indeed, the legislature had been debating an endless parade of bills with the sole purpose of reinforcing the legal structure of segregation. Henry B.'s twenty-two-hour filibuster served to kill off most of the offensive legislation. "I seek to register the plaintive cry," he spoke, lifting his arms in a gesture of pleading, "… the silent, the dumb protest of the inarticulate…"

Henry B. had been born in San Antonio in 1916, his parents having immigrated from Mexico during the Mexican Revolution. For almost the entire first half of his life he was subjected to a kind of discrimination that might surprise many in modern-day America; the second portion of Henry B.'s life became a crusade to assure that what happened to him would never again be perpetrated upon others in this country.

Growing up as a kid, he saw white-sheeted klansmen riding through the Mexican neighborhoods. Though his family wasn't poor ("We had books on the shelves"), he was still forced to attend a far inferior "Mexican school." Likewise, Henry B. could not go to public restaurants, movie theaters, barbershops, swimming pools, etc., because of the color of his skin.

Not knowing English held Henry B. back in the first grade, yet he would go on to speak four languages and read prolifically all his life. In second grade, he was to experience a remarkable awakening. "My wonderful, inspiring teacher, Miss Mason, made it clear that if we were born in the United States, we were Americans. This was astonishing news because at home we were being brought up as Mexicans who would eventually go back to the homeland. That evening at the supper table I announced this startling revelation: I am an American because I was born here. My aunt said, 'Well, if that's so, if a cat is born in an oven does that make him bread?' I was laughed out of the room. 'Ha, ha, he wants to make believe he is a gringo.'"

Yet maintaining his proud Mexican heritage while merging it with a new American identity, both fueled by education, provided Henry B. with a time-honored pathway out of the ghetto and into the mainstream of American life. He was a liberal Democrat in the largest sense of those words, i.e., he always stood up for the people against special interests and big corporations. In other words, he represented the little fellers, not the Rockefellers. Just as he had implied in his successful Texas Senate filibuster against segregation, he would become a voice for those who didn't have one.

In 1961, Henry B. became the first Mexican American to be elected to the United States Congress where he represented Texas' 20th Congressional District for thirty-eight years. He served with passion, eloquence, and integrity and, unlike many other long-serving political personages, he never forgot from whence he came. He was never a saint; he was a fighter. And he fought for those who'd grown up on the wrong side of every American town.

Even though he was chairman of the Banking Committee, he lived entirely on his salary, steadfastly refusing to take contributions from special interests that might have been affected by his positions of power in the Congress. From desegregating public swimming pools when he served on the San Antonio City Council, to his passionate stand against the hateful agenda of the 1957 legislature (eight out of ten bills were defeated), to his thirty-seven years in Congress Henry B. sold out to no one. He never forgot what life was like in the barrio, and he led the way in the slow, grudging, painful battle against discrimination in all its forms and devices.

Before they called them "focus groups," Henry B. had his own. They were the people he associated with and never lost touch with – the barbers, gas station attendants, postal workers, waitresses, plumbers, electricians, and neighbors. And he never forgot his best friend's mother, the kind lady who'd gone blind from sewing baby clothes by hand for five cents a piece. These were Henry B.'s people and their spirit guided him on the homefront and in the halls of Congress.

Wanda "Fluffy" Cash, a friend of mine, was one of Henry B.'s neighbors for many years in San Antonio. "He would come back from Washington as much as possible," she said. "You could always tell when the Congressman was in town because he'd be out there mowing his lawn. He invariably wore black socks, business shoes, and Bermuda shorts. It always impressed me that he mowed his own lawn."

Henry B. was not only a fighter for the rights of the downtrodden. He was a fighter, period. He believed that if you respected yourself, others would respect you as well. "I was always in the minority," he once said, "even when I was in the majority."

When he was in his early seventies, some guy at another table at Earl Abel's restaurant in San Antonio called him a communist. Henry B. got up from his chair and promptly walked over and decked the much younger man. Henry B. claimed at the time that, although he'd been the one who'd been provoked, he'd acted in a fairly restrained manner. "If I'd acted out of passion," he said, "that fellow would still not be able to eat chalupas."

Juan Seguin
The Paul Revere of Texas

On a chilly night in late February 1836, a young Tejano rider named Juan Seguin threaded his way stealthily through the Mexican army encampment. His mission was a final desperate appeal from Travis for reinforcements at the Alamo. Juan, who'd been elected alcalde (mayor) of Bexar, had led a group of Tejanos into the old mission to fight alongside the Anglos for Texas independence against the ruthless Mexican dictator Santa Anna. Juan might not have known it then, but he was the last man to leave the Alamo.

It is not surprising that Juan's sympathies lay with the Texians; his father, Erasmo Seguin, had traveled about the United States extensively and had come to love its freedom, prosperity, and democracy. Erasmo bought land near what is now Floresville and built a house he called Casa Blanca. The elder Seguin had become good friends with Stephen F. Austin and became a key player when Moses Austin died and left things to his son, Stephen. Mexico had won its independence from Spain and this necessitated Austin's colony to renegotiate the deal Moses had made with Spain. Erasmo helped young Stephen get permission from Mexico to continue the colony. Juan not only had a family history of friendship with the colonists, he was a native himself, having been born in San Antonio.

Now, as Juan rode through the night toward Goliad, he was well aware that Colonel James Fannin's cooperation was essential if the Texians were to be saved at the Alamo. He had also brought eight Tejano friends into the Alamo to fight alongside the Anglos, and their fates must have weighed upon him as well. When he got to Goliad, however, he could not convince Fannin to come to the aid of the men trapped at the Alamo. (Fannin would eventually surrender with more than three hundred and sixty of his men put to death at the orders of Santa Anna. Fannin himself wrote a note requesting he be shot in the chest in a dignified fashion and his gold watch sent to his family back home. The Mexicans shot him in the face, threw him on a stack of burning bodies, and a Mexican soldier took his gold watch.)

Juan rode on to the ranches along the lower Guadalupe and San Antonio Rivers, enlisting Tejanos from amongst the vaqueros and rancheros. He and his small force met up with newly appointed General Sam Houston at Gonzales. It was there that they got the bad news: The Alamo had fallen. Like he was to do at Goliad, the bloody dictator had ordered them all put to death.

General Sam knew his small, ragged army was not ready to take on Santa Anna. He ordered the town of Gonzales burned to keep it from providing shelter to Santa Anna, who was moving eastward, threatening to drive all Anglos out of Texas. General Sam knew that if he was to come up with a new army he would have to do it with the settlers along the Brazos from Austin's colony. He gave Juan Seguin the orders to ride to all the remote villages and farms along the frontier to warn them all of Santa Anna's

threatening advance, and recruit all able-bodied men into the Texas army.

Because of Juan's success at enlisting new men for the army and warning the settlers of their imminent peril, he became known as the Paul Revere of Texas. All women and non-combatants headed en masse eastward to cross the border into the United States. This vast and sudden exodus became known as the Runaway Scrape. Most of the men Juan alerted, however, eagerly joined up with General Sam. What followed was a cat-and-mouse game all across the flooded and muddy countryside until the Mexican army and the Texas army both finally arrived at their fated destination – the point at which the San Jacinto River met Buffalo Bayou.

General Sam was now preparing to do battle with the much larger Mexican army. Juan had organized a company of Tejanos to fight alongside the Anglos but the general forcefully opposed the idea. Instead, he ordered Juan and his troops to remain behind the battlelines and guard the supplies. After the cruel massacre of the prisoners at the Alamo and Goliad, he was worried that some in the Texas army might do harm to Juan and his men because they were of Mexican descent.

Juan was deeply insulted. He wanted his Tejano company to fight on the lines with the rest of the army. It is a measure of what high regard the general had for Juan that he rescinded the order and permitted the Tejano troops to fight in the battle. In order to prevent Juan's men from being shot at by mistake, it was determined that they would wear distinctive cardboard markers in their hatbands.

The battle itself was over in less than eighteen minutes. Juan and his troops performed gallantly. Juan himself accepted the surrender of many

Mexican officers, most of whom begged him to spare their lives, which, unlike Santa Anna, he did. (It wasn't difficult to spot the Mexican officers; they were the only ones on the entire battlefield who had uniforms.) Juan, who'd been promoted to Captain by Stephen F. Austin, was now promoted to Lt. Colonel by David G. Burnet, the President of the Republic of Texas.

Almost exactly a year from the time he rode forth from the Alamo to attempt to get reinforcements, Juan returned to that sacred, doomed mission to supervise the final ceremonial burial of the last remains of its brave defenders. When Juan died in Nuevo Laredo in 1890, his body was buried in Mexico. But on July 4, 1976, with both governments working together, his remains were removed and ceremonially re-buried under a beautiful grove of live oak trees in the Texas city that now bears his name.

J. Frank Dobie
Defender of the Strays

"They call me a folklorist," J. Frank Dobie once wrote, "but I am not a scientific folklorist. After I have heard a story, I do all I can to improve it."

However he did it, it must be said that J. Frank Dobie taught Texans, and spiritual Texans, more than any other man of his time about their landscape, cultural history, environment, and the animals they shared the land with. From tiny hummingbirds to the Texas Longhorn breed of cattle – which Dobie is credited with saving from extinction – he loved all creatures great and small, especially those who lived in the wild.

Dobie recognized that the rich experiences of rural living and Texas ranch life were vanishing before his eyes in his home state. His myriad stories, pamphlets, and books helped to revive a way of life to many who'd lived it and lost it, and introduced the spirit of the American Southwest to people around the world. He was not merely a folklorist; he was a pro-active folklorist, a poet, and a literary man with few if any pretensions.

A friend of J. Frank's, at his funeral in 1964, described him in quite a beautiful and accurate way. "He was a stray and a defender of strays," said the friend. The people and the animals, he believed, had a certain linkage whether or not they knew or appreciated it. They were both victims of the terrible tracks of progress across J. Frank's beloved Southwest. He was an eloquent spokesman for animals as well as for human beings.

Part of him was a biologist; part of him was a cultural anthropologist; and part of him was a teacher, a dreamer, and a creator. He was also, of course, a brilliant story-teller, whose tales reached out to entertain, educate, enlighten, as well as show us another way to live on this planet. Like Ladybird Johnson, he was an environmentalist before anyone really knew the meaning of the word. That put him ahead of his time. It also put him at odds with the powers that be at the University of Texas, and indeed, the State of Texas.

One would not think a mere story-teller or folklorist could stir up as much trouble as Dobie managed to do in his lifetime, but that's what sometimes happens when someone clearly and forcefully demonstrates the human qualities of animals and the animal nature of humans. It is difficult to be a defender of strays without becoming one. Thus, Dobie had a love-hate relationship with his long-time employer, the University of Texas, and crossed swords regularly with most of the politicians of his day. "When I get ready to explain homemade fascism in America," he once wrote, "I can take my example from the state capitol of Texas."

J. Frank's spirit, politically, culturally, spiritually, was as wild as the animals and the people and the landscapes he loved. He wrote often about the mustangs and the men who caught and trained them. One of his subjects was an African American mustanger, a former slave, named Bob Lemmons. "He was the most original mustanger I ever met. He always mustanged alone. After locating a bunch, he made no effort to keep up with the horses. He followed tracks. After he began following a herd of mustangs, he changed

neither horse nor clothing until he led the herd into a pen. This was to keep the mustangs from getting a 'foreign' scent. Within a week the herd he was after would usually allow him to direct their course."

J. Frank spun a web of magic over the people and the animals and the places he wrote about, making readers and listeners wish they could have been there. Many years ago, when I was a college student at the same university that dismissed J. Frank, I recall reading a story in one of his books that has stayed with me through the years. It was about him driving through Oklahoma in the forties and coming to an old trading post beside the highway.

He got out of his car and wandered around to the back and saw an old rusted cage. He looked inside and saw a beautiful golden eagle whose head had been bloodied from trying to get out. The cage was smaller than the majestic bird's wingspan and J. Frank felt a great impulse to free the imprisoned animal. He noticed the hasp on the cage and saw that there was no lock, only a piece of rusted wire keeping the cage door closed. It would only take moments to open the door but he hesitated. He walked around to see if anyone was watching. By the time he got back to the cage, the man who ran the trading post had come out.

The man looked suspiciously at J. Frank. After some discussion, he offered to sell him the eagle for three hundred dollars that J. Frank didn't have. At last, he drove away with a heavy heart, realizing if he'd acted on his first instinct the eagle might be free.

Years later, he retraced his journey, but now the eagle and the trading post were gone. Indeed, even the highway had been replaced by a new superhighway. Yet the eagle still flew in his consciousness. He knew he would carry the eagle in his soul until the day he died. Writing about it now seems almost tragic, but reading J. Frank's account makes one realize that the only things one ever really keeps are the things we let slip through our fingers.

On September 14, 1964, four days before he died, J. Frank Dobie was awarded the Medal of Freedom by the President of the United States. Whatever had become of his eagle, J. Frank must have known they would both soon be free. His own words from his book, *The Mustangs*, eloquently capture the spirit of J. Frank Dobie.

"So sometimes yet, in the realities of silence and solitude,

For a few people unhampered a while by things,

The mustangs walk out with dawn, stand high, then

Sweep away, wild with sheer life, and free, free, free –

Free of all confines of time and flesh!"

Emily Morgan
The Yellow Rose of Texas

Let no one call Emily Morgan an unsung heroine; every time you hear "The Yellow Rose of Texas," think of it as a lasting tribute to the slave girl who helped Sam Houston win the Texas Revolution.

Her story begins in 1830 when a wealthy businessman from Philadelphia, James Morgan, came to the Mexican colony of Texas for the cheap land values and the business opportunities. Morgan had sixteen slaves and one of them was the beautiful, longhaired mulatto, Emily. Interestingly enough, Mexico in some ways was more progressive than the United States at that time. It did not permit slavery in its territories. Thus James Morgan made his slaves into ninety-nine-year indentured servants, paying them one hundred dollars a year, and effectively getting around the law. Very likely to avoid the prejudice against mixed-race people, Emily volunteered to be indentured and to come to Texas. As was the custom of the day, she took the last name of the owner.

James Morgan had laid out the settlement of New Washington, which was near the mouth of the San Jacinto River. The place where the land reached out into the bay was called Morgan's Point. Morgan had been assigned to guard the port of Galveston and command Fort Travis. This

was vital because it meant keeping the supply lines open for Sam Houston's tiny, rag-tag army. On the morning of April 16, 1836, James Morgan was in Galveston and Emily had been left in New Washington with the task of loading the boats that were intended to supply the Texian troops.

The Mexican cavalry arrived in New Washington just in time to miss capturing President David G. Burnet who got away to Galveston Island on a schooner. They then turned their sights on Morgan's warehouse and noticed the graceful mulatto girl loading the boats. Emily was taken prisoner along with other servants and workmen. Two days later, Santa Anna himself marched into a mostly deserted New Washington and was reportedly instantly taken with Emily's grace and beauty. The Mexican dictator was already married to two different women at the time, but he fashioned himself as "the Napoleon of the West," and, like all dictators, believed no laws were meant for him. His men looted, pillaged, and burned what was left of the settlement, and then Santa Anna took his own spoils of war, Emily and a young printer's apprentice named Turner.

Documents of the time describe Turner as a "yellow boy," meaning mixed race like Emily herself, like "The Yellow Rose of Texas." Santa Anna, however, had plans for both of them. He would make the boy take his men to Sam Houston's camp. And he would take Emily back with him to his fancy octagonal tent replete with a piano, silk sheets, champagne, silver serving dishes, crystal goblets, an opium cabinet, and a state-of-the-art mounted sterling chamber pot. Emily, however, had other ideas.

She was able to persuade the young boy, who was an excellent horseman, to elude Santa Anna's scouts and ride to Houston's encampment to inform the general of Santa Anna's arrival. Young Turner did precisely what Emily had instructed him to do, enabling Houston to surreptitiously move his men to within a mile of Santa Anna's headquarters. Santa Anna was so eager to spend some time alone with Emily that he ordered his troops to encamp along the plains of the San Jacinto. The location of the encampment, his officers argued, was a poor one strategically. It left the men vulnerable to attack. Santa Anna would hear none of it, however. He had other ideas, too.

On the morning of April 21, a fateful day indeed, Sam Houston and his chief scout, Deaf Smith, found a high ridge, climbed a tree, and were actually able to get a few glimpses into the lavish three-room tent in which Emily and the Mexican general were sequestered. "I hope that slave girl makes him neglect his business," Sam reportedly said, "and keeps him in bed all day." They watched as Emily served breakfast to Santa Anna as he sat at the table wearing his bright red silk houserobe.

At approximately 4:00 p.m. that afternoon Sam Houston and the tiny Texas army attacked. The event was recorded by a visiting Englishman, William Bollaert, who described the affair as follows: "The Battle of San Jacinto was probably lost to the Mexicans owing to the influence of a Mulatta Girl (Emily) belonging to Colonel Morgan, who was closeted in the tent with General Santana, at the time the cry was made, 'The enemy! They come! They come!' (She) detained Santana so long that order could not be restored readily again."

The battle was over in less than eighteen minutes. The count on the battlefield was six hundred and thirty Mexicans killed, two hundred and eight wounded, and seven hundred and thirty taken prisoner. According to

General Rusk, Sam Houston's forces numbered seven hundred and fifty with only two Texans killed and seven who died later from injuries suffered on the battlefield. Santa Anna himself was captured the next day. He was literally caught with his pants down. Instead of his customary sartorial finery, he was barefoot, wearing coarse white laborers' pants and a large serape to cover his diamond-studded silk shirt. Though almost everyone wanted him dead, Sam Houston spared his life.

As far as Emily's story goes, history is unclear. Colonel James Morgan was so impressed with her heroic actions that he gave her her freedom, a home near what would become Houston, and a ticket back to New York if she wished to go back there. The public probably never would have heard Emily's story if a library in Chicago hadn't acquired William Bollaert's diary almost ninety years later. It wasn't until the 1950s that excerpts were finally published and the world learned what Sam Houston, Colonel James Morgan, and William Bollaert already knew – that Emily Morgan played a key role in Texas gaining her independence from Mexico.

Perhaps cosmically, Mitch Miller's big hit version of "The Yellow Rose of Texas" came out at about the same time as Bollaert's historical references to Emily. Though the lyrics have changed, the song has been around since early slave times and the true meaning of the title remains unknown to many fans of what has become one of the most enduring melodies ever written.

There are a growing number of historians and others, however, who do take the song to be a tip of the hat to the mixed-race slave girl who, by her quick and courageous actions, may well have saved Texas. Though no one knows what became of the real Emily Morgan, the Knights of the Yellow Rose of Texas honor her memory reverently each April 21st at San Jacinto. Also the historic Emily Morgan Hotel was named in her honor in San Antonio. It is nestled, appropriately, close to the Alamo.

James Bonham

The Messenger

On the morning of March 3, 1836, James Butler Bonham stood on a hill overlooking the little town of San Antonio. He had been riding back the ninety-five miles from Goliad at somewhat slower than the breakneck pace he'd traveled there; no one likes to be the bearer of bad news. Fannin and his four hundred man fighting force – the largest in Texas at the time – would not be coming to the aid of the men of the Alamo any time soon. Then, just outside the city, James had heard the cannon booming and he knew that soon might already be too late.

Below him he could see the Mexican army intensifying its fire on the Alamo. Another courier on the hill with him tried to reason with the brash twenty-nine-year-old South Carolinian. Don't go down there, he'd said to James. You'll face certain death. But there was no place else to go, thought James. What was the point in seeking out Sam Houston and his non-existent army? And this was the second time he'd carried Travis' desperate message to Fannin with no results. There would be no reinforcements coming to the aid of the men in the Alamo. Travis was his boyhood friend and he wanted to tell him that in person.

History has not been kind to Fannin. In truth, he had started out for

the Alamo on February 28, but an ox cart broke down not far out of Goliad and Fannin's will broke down with it. He led his men back to Goliad, where he surrendered, and, on March 27, Palm Sunday, proceeded to watch the Mexican army, at Santa Anna's specific orders, murder his men and himself.

James Bonham had come a long way to reach this hilltop. In 1833, as a lawyer in Pendleton, South Carolina, he'd beaten another lawyer with a cane for insulting his female client in court. When the judge reprimanded James, instead of saying, "I'm sorry, your honor," he told the judge he'd like to "tweak his nose." The judge gave James ninety days for contempt of court.

But the women of Pendleton loved James for his gallantry, a trait that would remain with him all his life. They brought special dishes and flowers to him in jail. He could have had any woman in town except one, and she was the woman he loved. She was unimpressed with his courtroom antics and persistent courtship on his part could not move her. Brokenhearted, he left town.

Following his true adventurer's soul and at the urgings of his friend Travis, James drifted to Texas. Travis had written him about the high hopes for independence, the trials and tribulations, the glory of Texas. "Stirring times are afoot here," Travis wrote. "Come on out to Texas and take a hand in affairs." Texas was a magnet for someone like James. He had an unbridled spirit that was courageous to recklessness; he was a daring horseman and a skilled swordsman; and, above all, he had an unswayable sense of honor to the highest degree, akin to men like Sam Houston.

Houston, indeed, was quite impressed with young James. After reaching Texas in November of 1835, the South Carolinian wrote to Houston offering his services and turning down all pay, lands, or rations in return. Houston knew this was a man among men. He recommended that James receive a promotion to major, stating, "His influence in the army is great, more so than some who would be generals." The men listened to him, Houston added.

James arrived at the Alamo on January 19, 1836, very likely in the company of James Bowie. With the exception of two trips to the outside world, seeking reinforcements for Travis, the Alamo would be his home for the rest of his life. Of all the great heroes who died there – Crockett, Travis, Bowie, and the rest – James Bonham's story has been especially romanticized over the years. This is partly because he was always seen as a gentle, thoughtful, loyal, and honorable man. But it is also true that, of all the defenders of the Alamo, James had the greatest opportunity to escape the palpable, impending doom that had gathered around the fragile little mission, smothering all hope. He was on the outside and a free man. Yet he chose to return.

Some historians believe that it was not all bad news he was carrying back to Travis. As well as Fannin's rejection, there was also a letter from Robert M. Williamson assuring Travis that help was on the way and urging him to hold out. The men of the Alamo, however, had heard this all before, and with the Mexican hoards now besieging the place, few if any of them held much hope that reinforcements would come in time.

Whether James believed Fannin or Williamson, we do not know. We do know that his actions that day became emblematic of the loyalty and courage of all the men of the Alamo. He became a shining symbol, a veritable mortal template for courage, loyalty, friendship, and honor. Sam Houston had not been wrong about James Bonham.

"Don't throw your life away," the other messenger on the hilltop beseeched James. From that vantage point, they both could clearly see the hopeless situation of his comrades. "I will report the result of my mission to Travis," James said, "or die in the attempt."

It was the afternoon of March 3, 1836, and James Bonham had three days to live. He rode down the hill and attached the agreed-upon white silk handkerchief to his hatband to alert Travis. Then he galloped past the legions of surprised Mexicans in broad daylight, dodging bullets as he went. Then he saw the gates of the Alamo open, and he rode through them into history.

Ralph Yarborough

Man of the People

In the narrow window between the Great Depression and the Great Society, Ralph W. Yarborough got an enormous amount accomplished for the people of our state and our nation. Preceded and followed by those on the far right, he is often remembered as "the patron saint of Texas liberals." Texas being essentially a one-party state at the time, Smilin' Ralph, as he was called, was routinely the victim of corrupt political machines and vicious smears from the right wing of the Democratic Party.

Ralph served in the United States Senate from 1957 to 1971 and during that time he was the only southern senator to vote for all civil rights bills including the Civil Rights Act of 1964 and the Voting Rights Act of 1965. He also co-wrote the Endangered Species Act. As a veteran himself, a Lt. Colonel who saw action in both the European and Pacific theaters of WWII, Smilin' Ralph worked to extend the G. I. Bill to cover cold war veterans as well, and fought corruption and bureaucracy in veterans affairs.

He not only stood up for the people of Texas, but, as an expert in land law, he prosecuted major oil companies for violating production limits or failing to pay oil royalties to the Permanent School Fund for drilling on public lands. He won the second-biggest judgment ever in Texas at that time, a million dollars from the Mid-Kansas Oil and Gas Company for not paying

oil royalties.

Ralph was one of the greatest environmentalists and conservationists Texas has ever produced. Though often unappreciated at the time, he was responsible for preserving as parkland such threatened areas as the Big Thicket, the Guadalupe Mountains, and Padre Island. He was an author of much Great Society legislation when Lyndon Johnson was president, including Medicare and Medicaid, federal support for higher education, the War on Poverty, and, of course, support for the veterans, who were always close to his heart.

With a broad and varied background in the real world, he was the kind of politician not often seen these days. He was a teacher, a soldier, a lawyer, and a judge, and he believed in old-fashioned politics, getting out there and shaking hands and meeting people. He was precisely the kind of populist that had made the Democratic Party so dominant in the past century. "Let's put the jam on the lower shelf," he was fond of saying, "so the little people can reach it."

As well as serving a long and distinguished career in the United States Senate (he was a highly unusual kind of southern senator, one of the very few not to sign the Southern Manifesto opposing integration), he also ran unsuccessfully three times for governor. Many observers today believe Ralph Yarborough was robbed on several occasions by the corrupt political machines of the right-wing of the Democratic Party. In 1954, after *Brown v. Board of Education*, the voices on the right became increasingly shrill and venomous. Governor Allan Shivers did everything he could to hold back integration. "We're going to keep the system that we know is best," he said. "No law, no court, can wreck what God has made." Shivers all but called

Yarborough a communist and said he was working "hand-in-glove with the NAACP."

The climate politically was toxic in Texas, especially for a smilin' liberal like Ralph, yet he remained a happy warrior. White Citizen's Councils sprang up in the summer of 1955, one of the few things we've borrowed from Mississippi. The Minute Women became a poisonous political force. They were so paranoid that they purposely kept no written bylaws and refused to permit motions from the floor at their meetings for fear that they might have been infiltrated by communists.

These right-wing hate groups, and many others like them, went after Ralph with a terrible vengeance, but he never gave up, and he never stopped smilin'. His theme song for all his campaigns was "The Yellow Rose of Texas," and I liked him for that, too. As a kid, I remember campaigning for him, rooting for him, pulling for him the way a young follower might have felt watching Socrates or Jesus lose their elections, as well. It was a crushing blow every time Ralph Yarborough lost, because I knew, even then, that he represented all that was good about Texas.

Ralph's Senate Office Building suite in Washington reportedly had all the usual trappings of a successful politician. All the awards, plaques, pictures of the senator with famous and powerful people were there, to be sure. (He may have been a teacher, soldier, lawyer, judge and an advocate for working people, the man who helped create and nurture such Texas trailblazers as Ann Richards and Jim Hightower, but he was also a politician. And that, too, was part of his charm.) For the centerpiece on the wall of his senate office was a subtle tribute of which the author may well have been unaware.

It was a ragged paragraph clipped from the *Austin American-Statesman* dated April 7, 1957. It read as follows: "A prominent local lobbyist stopped in at Ralph Yarborough's campaign headquarters on Congress Avenue on election night. Talking to newsmen at the Capitol, he spoke wonderingly of what he'd seen. 'It was fantastic,' he muttered. 'There wasn't a big shot down there! Nothing but people!'"

John Henry Faulk

Fear on Trial

John Henry was born in 1913 in Austin and grew up in South Austin to middle-class Methodist parents. They were free thinking people and taught him to detest racism and to have a liberated mind. As a result, as he grew older, he hung out with poor black neighbors and colorful, rather earthy cedar choppers instead of middle-class Methodists.

He always had a knack for mimicry and story telling and these skills became increasingly honed under the tutelage of one of his professors at the University of Texas, J. Frank Dobie. John Henry recorded and analyzed ten sermons from African-American churches along the Brazos River for his Master's thesis. His research confirmed his belief that minorities faced grave challenges at the time when it came to civil rights.

In the early forties, John Henry taught English at the university, often employing story telling and mimicry to explore the best and the worst of Texas culture and customs. He told tall tales, bawdy jokes, and had an uncanny ability to parody and praise human behavior. There was, unfortunately, not a great demand for this in academia. So, when the war came, even though the army rejected him for a bad eye, he nonetheless joined the Merchant Marines, then the Red Cross, and then got into the army as a medic.

Radio gave John Henry's talents the showcase they needed to reach the audience he deserved. Through his friend Alan Lomax, he got his first weekly CBS radio show in 1946, "Johnny's Front Porch." For the next five years, he climbed the ladder rapidly in the popular world of radio, which dominated the American media of the day. Then, on December 17, 1951, "The John Henry Faulk Show" debuted on WCBS. The show featured political humor, listener participation, and music, and ran very successfully for six years. Rumors flew in the industry and in the media that John Henry was on his way to soon becoming one of the biggest stars in American entertainment.

And then, suddenly, incredibly, it all came to an end. John Henry had been "blacklisted." He had been branded a communist by a group called AWARE, Inc., an ultra-patriotic, for-profit company that ruined careers on a regular basis in those days of cold war politics. John Henry was unfairly made a victim, but he was a victim who would fight back.

"Blacklisting," John Henry explained, "was the term used to describe the practise of systematically denying employment to persons for their alleged political beliefs and associations. It was just one of a multitude of cruel manifestations of the McCarthy era in the United States, a period of years in the 1950s characterized by widespread persecution and repression.

"Senator Joe McCarthy of Wisconsin sailed over the national horizon in 1950, using the charges of treason and subversion to intimidate his political opponents into quaking silence. Hence 'McCarthyism' entered our political lexicon.

"The climate of fear and hysteria that invaded our political institutions... was carefully encouraged and orchestrated by governmental

bodies as well as by private groups. In Congress, the House Un-American Activities Committee; in the Senate, the Internal Security Committee; and, in the Executive Branch, J. Edgar Hoover's FBI kept up a steady drumbeat of alarms and exposures. Self-appointed private groups like the American Legion and AWARE, Inc., joined the clamor and din.

"That respected maxim of American justice which says that a person charged with a crime is presumed innocent until proven guilty by due process of the law was stood on its head and became 'a person charged with holding dissenting views is presumed guilty until proven innocent.'"

John Henry was not intimidated; he hired New York attorney Louis Nizer and took AWARE, Inc., to court. CBS News vice-president Edward R. Murrow helped finance the effort and supported John Henry in trying to end blacklisting. Though the suit was filed in 1957, it was stalled for five years. Finally, on June 28, 1962, the jury awarded John Henry the largest libel judgment in history to that date, $3.5 million. An appeals court cut that to $500,000, which disappeared, in legal fees and debts.

In 1963, John Henry published a book, *Fear on Trial*, about his legal fight with AWARE, which was made into a movie version in 1974 by CBS. But CBS never rehired him. He came back to Austin in 1968 and continued to speak out about First Amendment rights, write and produce plays, and, from 1975 to 1980, portray a popular homespun character on the television hit *Hee-Haw*.

John Henry was never known as a bitter man, but the blacklist had cynically and effectively destroyed his blameless reputation and skyrocketing career, all in the phony rhetoric of patriotism. What happened to John Henry

Faulk is a tragedy of American proportions that Americans must never allow to happen again. Yet, by challenging these evil forces, he helped expose the blacklist for what it was, and the people behind it for the cowards they were. As Studs Terkel later observed, "He faced the bastards and beat them down."

Today John Henry is remembered as not just a story-teller but as a truth-teller, a man who fought and won one of the great civil rights battles of the twentieth century. For the specter of McCarthyism and the blacklist represent one of the darkest chapters in American political, social, and cultural history. It is a past that we can never be sure is truly past. Yet today, the liars, demagogues, cowards, and false patriots who attacked John Henry are namelessly buried under the shameful rubric of McCarthyism. And today as well, very fittingly, the downtown branch of the Austin library is named the John Henry Faulk Public Library.

In the end it is clear that John Henry was never a communist; he was, perhaps, something far more dangerous. He was a humorist. Here is what Governor Ann Richards had to say about his legacy: "During his life, John Henry Faulk had that 'homespun philosopher' image. Underneath that country-boy talk, however, lay a razor sharp wit and keen mind. John Henry exhibited conviction, compassion, timeless wisdom, and wonderful talent. He also had that special way of separating the wheat from the chaff, and making us see our own foolishness. Through humor, he made us examine our prejudices."

Lady Bird Johnson

First Lady

In May of 1930 Lady Bird was gazing dreamily out the window of the plane as the charming little town of Austin came into view. She had just graduated from St. Mary's Episcopal College for Women in Dallas and she was kind of at loose ends. A girlfriend from Marshall was planning to attend the University of Texas and had asked her to come along and so she had. She was interested in journalism or maybe she would become a teacher. She was a very intelligent girl but a little bit on the shy side, and the University of Texas seemed like a daunting challenge to someone from the little East Texas town of Karnack.

Then the plane dropped lower in preparation for landing. Suddenly, Lady Bird saw a beautiful field of bluebonnets stretching out across the landscape as far as the eye could see. It would be a prophetic welcome to one whose life was about to be changed forever in so many ways. It was also a reminder of who she was and where she'd come from, of a childhood spent quite often alone, but always close to nature.

Lady Bird fell in love with Austin. She registered at the university and in 1933 received a Bachelor of Arts degree with honors and, in 1934, a second bachelor's degree cum laude in journalism. She also earned a teaching certificate. Lady Bird accomplished these things at a time when very few women had a college education, much less, a career of their own. Her dream was to become a reporter. But what good are dreams if they come true?

That summer, after graduation, Lady Bird and a girlfriend of hers visited Washington, D.C. At one point they found themselves at 1600 Pennsylvania Avenue, just peering whimsically through the fence at the White House. Like the field of bluebonnets, it was to be a prophetic experience.

Her plans to be a reporter were suddenly sidetracked in Austin when she met Lyndon Baines Johnson, a young, brash, political aide to Congressman Richard Kleberg. Their first date was breakfast the next morning at the historic Driskill Hotel. After breakfast, Lyndon took Lady Bird for a long, leisurely drive in the country, during which, amazingly, he proposed to her.

Lady Bird did not want to rush things. Indeed, at first she thought he was joking. Lyndon, however, was very confident and persistent. As she told one of her girlfriends later, he was "a young man in a hurry." This kind of rash decision though, was not in keeping with Lady Bird's style. She wanted Lyndon, at the very least, to meet her father. Lyndon agreed, and she took him to Karnack.

Lady Bird's father, Thomas Jefferson, or T. J. Taylor, was a farmer and merchant who called himself "Dealer in Everything." He had married Lady Bird's mother much against her parents' wishes, who believed that he was "nothing but a dirt farmer." It might even be said that T. J. had "married up" just as Lyndon was attempting to do. So, after introducing the two men and letting them get acquainted for a time, Lady Bird asked her dad if he didn't think they might be rushing the marriage plans a bit. But T. J. was

favorably impressed with the young politician. "Some of the best trades I ever made," he said, "were done in a hurry."

Less than two months later Lady Bird accepted Lyndon's proposal, and on November 17, 1934, they were married at St. Mark's Episcopal Church in San Antonio. The only problem was that in his excitement Lyndon had forgotten to buy a ring. The best man rushed out to the nearest store he could find and managed to purchase a wedding ring for $2.98. Lady Bird wore that ring for thirty-six years until President Johnson one day asked the First Lady why she'd never replaced the cheap ring with a nicer one. "Why, darling," she said, "I was waiting to see if the marriage lasted."

Not only did the marriage last but Lady Bird never lost her close, personal relationship with nature. She was an environmentalist before we even had the word. As First Lady she was an advocate for wildflowers, rivers, national and state parks, old groves of trees, animals in the wild, and leaving the land in a more beautiful condition than we'd found it. Her enemies were billboards, shopping centers, pollution, strip-mining and a myriad of other things that brought about the desecration of the natural beauty of the country. "The little girl on Caddo Lake," wrote historian Lewis Gould, "had come far from the flowers and fields of East Texas, but she never lost the sense of kinship with the land and its natural beauty. When her opportunity came to be an advocate for the preservation and perpetuation of the nation's environment, she seized it with dedication, commitment, and lasting results."

Both for residents and tourists alike, Lady Bird supervised the planting of millions of flowers in our nation's capital. "Where flowers bloom," she said, "so does hope." Her efforts to protect wildflowers and sponsor the planting of them along highways throughout the country inspired many similar programs all over America. The Highway Beautification Act, or "Lady Bird's Bill" as it was sometimes called, planted, landscaped, and beautified roadside parks and areas near highways, and limited billboards. She was the first woman to serve on the National Geographic's Board of Trustees and she also served on the National Park Service Advisory Board.

On her seventieth birthday, she co-founded (with actress Helen Hayes) the National Wildflower Research Center near Austin. Devoted to reintroducing native plants and preserving them in planned landscapes, this nonprofit organization won Lady Bird the nickname of "the Johnny Appleseed of Wildflowers." After she died, in 2007, Austin's Town Lake was renamed Lady Bird Lake, for all her efforts to save and beautify the riverfront.

Carroll Abbott of Kerrville was one of the most learned and passionate wildflower advocates in the state. When Lady Bird founded the National Wildflower Research Center, she planted seeds from Carroll's company. He was the expert Lady Bird most often relied upon when it came to wildflowers.

Carroll often claimed that for years no one seemed concerned about wildflower survival. "Only God and Lady Bird Johnson," he added, "and not necessarily in that order."

Davy Crockett

King of the Wild Frontier

Davy wasn't born in Texas but he got here as fast as he could. Unlike James Bonham, he was not singularly motivated by the notion of helping Texas in the fight for her independence. Davy, instead, was seeking a second start in life. He was a politician who'd had enough of politics, a celebrity who'd seen enough of fame. When he lost his congressional seat to a peg-legged lawyer, he made the following famous statement to his former constituents, "Since you have chosen to elect a man with a timber toe to succeed me, you may all go to hell and I will go to Texas."

Davy was pushing fifty, making him one of the oldest men at the Alamo, certainly the most famous, and giving him a license to be a bit cynical about politics and life. And yet Davy had his dreams. He saw Texas as a place where he might possibly rekindle his somewhat weather-beaten political reputation as well as accomplish something he'd tried and failed to do his entire life, garner a comfortable measure of wealth for himself and his family.

There is no question that Davy loved what he saw of Texas. On January 9, 1836, he wrote his last surviving letter to his children, "I must say as to what I have seen of Texas, it is the garden spot of the world," he wrote. "The best land and the best prospects for health I ever saw, and I do believe

it is a fortune to any man to come here. There is a world of country here to settle… I have taken the oath of government and have enrolled my name as a volunteer and will set out for the Rio Grand in a few days with the volunteers from the United States. But all volunteers is entitled to vote for a member of the convention or to be voted for, and I have but little doubt of being elected a member to form a constitution for this province. I am rejoiced at my fate. I had rather be in my present situation than to be elected to a seat in Congress for life. I am in hopes of making a fortune yet for myself and family, bad as my prospect has been."

While Davy may not have come to Texas to join the revolution, there is no doubt that he was the kind of man who would never have shied away from a fight. He liked a good fight. But it was also time for visions and revisions. Historians will always disagree about Davy. Based on his letter to his children, one would have to say that he saw Texas as a second beginning in life. Historians, moreover, are merely observers of life; Davy Crockett was a participant of life, the very spice of life, who, even in death, continues to give historians, as well as all the rest of us, something brave and different and beautiful to observe.

Destiny brought Davy to San Antonio de Bexar on February 9, 1836; the Mexican dictator Santa Anna arrived a mere eleven days later. As much as Davy found wrong and corrupt with the political process, he could not escape its muddy undercurrents. Travis had already disobeyed Houston's order to withdraw from the Alamo. Houston was a very close friend of President Jackson, a political enemy of Davy's. It might have been a natural thing for Davy to side with Travis. Or perhaps he was merely passing through and, like a good Samaritan, chose to align himself with the obvious underdog. All we can say for certain is that Davy was larger than life when he came to Texas, and after the Battle of the Alamo, he belonged to the ages.

Some in Washington had thought Davy a joke because of his outlandish frontier outfit and homespun, often comic style. Davy, however, was a serious soul with an impeccable moral compass. His personal watchword always was, "Be sure you're right – then go ahead!" And, in spite of his tall tales and wild ways, his essence was rooted in a quiet humility. When Davy first arrived at the Alamo, Travis wished to give him the rank of colonel. Indeed, Davy had been a colonel in the Tennessee militia. But Davy declined the rank, stating that he preferred to be a private. "Here I am, Colonel," he reportedly told Travis. "Assign me to some place and me and my Tennessee boys will defend it all right."

Travis' diary reports that when the first heavy bombardment came, "Crockett was everywhere in the Alamo, animating the men to do their duty." As one of the greatest sharpshooters in the world, other reports indicate that Davy and his trusty hunting rifle killed five Mexican gunners in succession as they each tried to fire a large cannon aimed at the Alamo. Some reports state as well that Davy also drew a bead on Santa Anna, who considered himself well out of reach of any conceivable rifle fire. It is said that Davy, firing from a virtually impossible distance, may have just missed taking the Mexican general out by mere inches.

Perhaps more than any man of his time, Davy's life and legend was then, and remains to this day, a mystifying mixture of fact and fiction. Sometimes, indeed, we can learn more about a person from the rich fiction that grows up around him than we can from the dry facts over which historians quibble. Davy at the Alamo was said to have played the fiddle, danced a jig, spun wild yarns, and out-drank just about anybody, and yet, when it came time to fight, he was an inspiration to every man.

That's the trouble with heroes; everyone tends to see them differently. Disney plays Davy one way, John Wayne, another, and Billy Bob Thornton, still another. Some historians claim that Davy, one of the most famous politicians in the country, had his eye on the White House. He knew that George Washington, whom he greatly admired, reached the presidency after winning the Revolutionary War. He knew that Jackson, whom he did not greatly admire, had won the presidency after winning the War of 1812. Did he think the Texas Revolution might do the same thing for him? Or, as many others feel, was he simply a stranger in a strange land, merely passing through, all the more poignant for fighting courageously a seemingly lost cause that wasn't even his own?

Did Davy die with a necklace of dead Mexicans lying in the dust all around him? Was he captured and shown no quarter by Santa Anna? No one really knows for sure. All we know is that the Alamo was one of the smaller missions in the province, but when Davy and his brave compatriots crossed Travis's line in the sand, knowing full well they were going to die, that was the moment when Texas was born.

Bigfoot Wallace
Folk Hero

The three most famous frontiersmen who ever set foot in Texas were Sam Houston, Davy Crockett, and Bigfoot Wallace. Sam was a politician who became a statesman. Davy was a politician who became a martyr and a legend. Bigfoot was not a politician at all; he was a big man with big feet who came from Virginia and evolved into a true folk hero.

While Sam and Davy came here to seek new beginnings, Bigfoot had quite another agenda. He came to Texas to avenge the murder of his brother at Goliad.

Like Davy, fact and fiction tended to blend together over time in the life of Bigfoot. Perhaps truth and half-truth are two of the necessary ingredients in the creation of a folk hero. Though Bigfoot is not as well known as Davy or Sam, his courage was so daring, and his genuine accomplishments so manifest, he belongs to posterity with them as a true architect of what made Texas great.

In October of 1837 Bigfoot arrived in Texas. The population of the state was estimated at 35,000 to 50,000, but Bigfoot instinctively sought out the extreme edge of the frontier, always finding his way from the settled places into the wilderness. He was individualistic, undisciplined, and very

dangerous if you were his enemy, but he was also said to be a jovial giant, forever on the lookout for a good laugh. He preferred water and buttermilk to whiskey or coffee.

He traveled from Galveston to Bastrop and then helped build the town of LaGrange. He went to the site of the Alamo in April 1838 and was shocked to see some of the ashes and small charred bones where the Mexicans had burned the bodies of the defenders. He collected them and buried them and made a vow that he would never be taken alive by the enemy. He thought of his brother without a weapon being slaughtered at Goliad. He'd told his father before he'd left Virginia that he planned to spend the balance of his time killing Mexicans.

He tried being a rancher and a farmer but soon came to the self-realization that he was born to be a frontiersman, a fighter of the enemies of Texas, be they Mexicans, Indians, or Anglo outlaws. And the enemies of Texas soon learned not to mess with Bigfoot.

In 1839 Bigfoot moved to Austin, the new capital of the Republic, and demonstrated his expertise with the broad-ax constructing buildings on both sides of Congress Avenue. The following year he went to San Antonio and applied for the Texas Rangers under Captain Jack Hays. Bigfoot's reputation had preceded him and he was signed up immediately. For the next few years he worked as a Ranger, scouting far and wide, fighting range wars, lawlessness of all kinds, horse thieves, bandits, and Comanche and Apache raiding parties.

In 1842 Bigfoot crossed the border with the ill-fated Mier Expedition and got his chance to get even with the Mexicans, though in the end, he was captured himself along with his greatly-outnumbered band of men. He was forced to participate in Santa Anna's infamous drawing of the black beans in Mexico City. Bigfoot drew a white bean cut of the jar and served two years in a Mexican prison, but seventeen of his compatriots drew black beans and were summarily executed by firing squad.

Bigfoot had worn out his moccasins during the long march to the jail and his feet had swelled up to twice their normal size. The Mexican bootmaker said, "Big man has big foot," and many believe that's where Bigfoot got his name. Some, however, claim he got the name earlier when trailing a three hundred pound Indian chief whose toe stuck out through a hole in his moccasin, making a unique track to follow. The chief was nicknamed Bigfoot and that moniker became forever attached to William Alexander Anderson Wallace as well.

When the United States went to war with Mexico in 1846, Bigfoot was at the front of the line to volunteer. He settled some old scores and was promoted to Captain in the Rangers. When the war ended, he came back to his cabin on the Medina River. He became a guide, protector, and Indian fighter, as he looked out for the settlers moving into the area. As the land became too crowded, however, he moved to a lonely, wild place east of the Hondo River and built his last cabin. He had a large, heavy rifle once belonging to James Bowie. He took the mail from San Antonio through the wild frontier to El Paso. He was the only man who could do it; everybody else who tried got killed or scared off by the Indians.

By the 1870s, Bigfoot settled down on his ranch for the most part. He lived alone with his horses, chickens, and his two beloved dogs, Sowder and Rock. He took the two dogs everyplace he went and when he had his meals, Sowder was on one side at the table and Rock was on the other. He would give them the choicest bites of everything he ate.

J. Frank Dobie in *Tales of Old-Time Texas* recounts just one of many colorful stories about Bigfoot and the Indians. Dobie claims Bigfoot was "too easygoing and openhearted to be vindictive." But sometimes the Indians were friendly and sometimes they were not. Most of the time they knew to leave Bigfoot alone, but one November night he was sleeping in his cabin west of the Medina River, and they slipped in and stole his horses.

Bigfoot went to the secret place where he kept his mare, saddled up, and went after them. His mare, incidentally, was named White Bean. According to Dobie, while tracking the Indians, he came upon a place where many hickory nuts had been blown to the ground in a storm. He put hundreds of them inside his shirt, pants, and hat until he looked like a western version of Santa Claus, and somehow managed to roll back on top of White Bean.

When Bigfoot got to their campsite, the Indians were already cooking and eating one of his horses. There were about forty of them. He managed to roll off White Bean, took aim, and soon there were thirty-nine. The Indians began firing arrows at Bigfoot with deadly accuracy but they all bounced off. Soon there was a pile of arrows all around him and a bunch of Comanches riding away as fast as they could go. Bigfoot got his horses and let the hickory nuts all fall to the ground. "You can kick me to death with grasshopper legs if a single, solitary hickory nut hadn't been split open," he later claimed. He gathered them all up and fed them to his pigs when he got home.

Bigfoot died at the age of eighty-two and was buried with full military honors in the State Cemetery in Austin. As I write this, the creek flowing by my old lodge is just visible from my window. It is a tributary of the Guadalupe River called Wallace Creek, named for Bigfoot Wallace, frontier scout. When other creeks and rivers in the Hill Country dry up in the times of drought, Wallace Creek always continues to flow strongly and sparkle in the sunshine.

Quanah Parker

Last Chief of the Comanches

In the spring of 1836 Texas was in turmoil. The Alamo had fallen. Then Goliad. Then came the remarkable and totally unexpected game-changer, the Battle of San Jacinto. But Texas was a big place and news traveled slowly. Cynthia Ann Parker, the blonde-haired, blue-eyed grand-daughter of a fundamentalist Baptist preacher, was nine years old on or about May 19, and may well not have known of these seminal events in the history of Texas. She was certainly unaware that she would soon become the most famous Indian captive in the western world.

Peta Nocona, the leader of the Comanche raiding party, eyed the isolated Fort Parker from the distance. The Elder John Parker, Cynthia's grandfather, had founded the "Hardshell" Baptist enclave two years earlier at a site approximately thirty-five miles east of present-day Waco. The Elder John Parker was a very ethnocentric man and he believed that everyone outside of Fort Parker was bound for hell. Subsequent events would prove that he was not entirely wrong.

Like a hawk, Peta Nocona swooped down with his band of Comanches upon the unprotected little fort. They killed and scalped John the Elder, raped his wife, pillaged the place, and took off for the hills with

Cynthia and her little brother John. The Parker children were greeted warmly by the Comanche Nation and soon felt more at home with them than they ever had in the white man's world.

In 1842, the Texas Rangers and the army of the Republic of Texas finally located John and brought him back to the Parkers. He was twelve and old enough to know he didn't want any part of "civilization." He promptly stole a horse and rode away looking for Cynthia and the tribe. He never found them and he never came back.

Cynthia soon received the Indian name Nadua, which meant "Someone Found." Not only did she never try to escape, but she also dyed her long blonde hair with mud and buffalo dung and kept her bright blue eyes deliberately downcast whenever strangers were around. She eventually married the warrior chief Peta Nocona and bore him three children, the eldest of whom, Quanah, would become the last of the Comanche warrior chiefs, and one of the greatest leaders of his people both in war and in peace.

By all reports, Quanah's little family survived and lived happily until December 17, 1860, when Cynthia was recaptured by Texas Rangers in the Battle of Pease River. Quanah, who may have been twelve or thirteen, was away hunting with the men when the Rangers stormed the campsite. By the time they returned, there were few alive to tell the story.

Apparently, Ranger Charles Goodnight, who discovered Cynthia, also saved her life. She tried to run with her baby Topsana ("Prairie Flower") in her arms, and Goodnight shouted, "Don't shoot! She's white!" When they finally captured her, all she told them was "Me, Cynthia."

They took her back to Fort Parker where she'd originally been captured more than twenty-five years before but, as the Parker family soon learned, she was not Cynthia Ann anymore. She repeatedly demanded to be sent back to her husband and her family and tried to escape so many times that a guard finally had to be posted. Topsana, highly susceptible to the diseases of the white man, died a few years later at the age of four. Cynthia starved herself to death in 1870 at the age of forty-three.

Quanah became the leader of the largest and most notorious band of Comanches, the Quahadi, who fought quite successfully against the whites and remained free when all the others had signed treaties. Indeed, Quanah never lost a battle to the white man. Nonetheless, it was a terrible time to be a Native American in America. The white man was destroying the buffalo, a string of forts were springing up all across the land, and previously unheard of diseases were suddenly decimating the Indians. As great a warrior as Quanah was, his most important gift to his people may have been his ability to safely lead the entire Comanche tribe along the treacherous path to the uncertain future that awaited them.

In 1875, having run out of food and provisions, and being relentlessly pressured by the army, the Quahadi Comanches surrendered at last and moved to southwestern Oklahoma onto a reservation. Quanah was named chief of all the Comanches and taught them how to survive financially in the white man's world. Even more important, he taught them how to survive spiritually by founding the Native American Church, the only truly American religion, other than the Latter Day Saints, which is based on Christianity. Virtually every Native American tribe in North America has since adopted the Native American Church. "The white man goes into his church and talks about

Jesus," Quanah said. "The Indian goes into his tipi and talks with Jesus."

Quanah was one of the only true heroes of his day who was actually born in Texas. He was extremely adept at navigating both the Comanche culture and the white man's world. He dressed and lived in an American style, but he always wore his hair long and in braids. He had five wives and twenty-five children. He became one of the wealthiest Indians in America and saw that his tribe also made wise investments with their money. He was well respected by both Indians and whites. He went on hunting trips with President Teddy Roosevelt and carried on a lengthy correspondence with Charles Goodnight, the man who had recaptured Quanah's mother. Goodnight was illiterate and dictated his letters to his wife. Quanah wrote him back in English.

Quanah, one of the fiercest Comanche war chiefs of his time, carried a picture of his mother and his little sister with him every day of his life. He had their graves moved to Fort Sill Cemetery in Oklahoma, and when he died, he was buried beside them.

Upon Quanah's tombstone is the following epitaph:

"Resting Here Until Day Breaks

And Shadows Fall and Darkness

Disappears is

Quanah Parker Last Chief of the Comanches

Born 1852

Died Feb. 23, 1911."

Abernethy, Francis E. *Legendary Ladies of Texas.* Dallas: E-Heart Press, 1981.

Anderson, Adrian N., Ph.D. *Texas & Texans.* Columbus, Ohio: Glemcoe, McGraw-Hill, 2003.

Barnes, Marian E., *Black Texans.* Austin: Eakin Press, 1996.

Burton, Michael C. *John Henry Faulk – A Biography.* Austin: Eakin Press, 1993.

Campbell, Randolph B. *Gone to Texas, A History of the Lone Star State.* New York: Oxford University Press, 2003.

Caro, Robert A., *The Path to Power – The Years of Lyndon Johnson.* New York: Alfred A. Knopf, 1983.

Carroll, H. Bailey, *Heroes of Texas.* Waco: Texian Press, 1964.

Crawford, Ann F. and Ragsdale, Crystal S., *Women in Texas.* Austin: State House Press, 1992.

Cox, Mike. *Texas Ranger Tales II.* Plano: Republic of Texas Press, 1999.

Davis, Joe Tom. *Legendary Texians Vol. II.* Austin: Eakin Press, 1985.

Dobie, J. Frank. *Tales of Old-Time Texas*. New York: Little, Brown & Company, 1928.

Dobie, J. Frank. *The Flavor of Texas*. Dallas: Dealey & Lowe, 1936.

Dobie, J. Frank. *The Mustangs*. Austin: Little, Brown & Company, 1952.

Erickson, John R. *Ace Reid, Cowpoke*. Perryton, Texas: Maverick Books, 1984.

Faulk, John Henry, *Fear on Trial*. Austin University of Texas Press, 1963.

Graham, Don. *No Name on the Bullet, A Biography of Audie Murphy*. New York: Penguin Group, 1989.

Groneman, William III. *David Crockett, Hero of the Common Man*. Forge, 2005.

Haley, James L. *Sam Houston*. Norman: University of Oklahoma Press, 2002.

Hardin, Stephen L. *Texian Iliad, A Military History of the Texas Revolution*. Austin: University of Texas Press, 1994.

Harrigan, Stephen. *The Gates of the Alamo*. Alfred Knopf, 2000.

Hendrickson, Kenneth E. Jr. *The Chief Executives of Texas*. College Station: Texas A&M University Press, 1995.

Hightower, Jim. *There's Nothing in the Middle of the Road But Yellow Stripes and Dead Armadillos.* New York: Harper Perennial Press, 1997.

Ivins, Molly. *Molly Ivins Can't Say That, Can She?* New York: Random House, 1991.

Jackson, Jack, ed. *Almonte's Texas.* Austin: Texas State Historical Association. University of Texas, 2003.

James, Marquis. *The Raven, A Biography of Sam Houston.* Austin: University of Texas Press, 1926.

Kennedy, Caroline, ed. *Profiles in Courage for Our Time.* New York: Hyperion Books, 2002.

Kennedy, John F. *Profiles in Courage.* New York: Harper & Row, 1955.

McCall, Brian. *The Power of the Texas Governor.* Austin: University of Texas Press, 2009.

Morehead, Richard. *50 Years in Texas Politics.* Austin: Eakin Press, 1982.

Phillips, William G. *Yarborough of Texas.* Washington D.C.: Acropolis Books, 1969.

Powell Exley, Jo Ella. *Frontier Blood, The Saga of the Parker Family.* College Station: Texas A&M University Press, 2001.

Rogers, Mary Beth. *Barbara Jordan, American Hero*. New York: Bantam Books, 1998.

Sizer, Mona D. *Texas Heroes, A Dynasty of Courage*. Plano: Republic of Texas Press, 2000.

Sowell, A. J. *Life of Bigfoot Wallace*. Austin: State House Press, 1989. (Originally published in 1899)

Updyke, Rosemary Kissinger. *Quanah Parker, Comanche Chief*. Gretna, LA.: Pelican Publishing Company, 1991.

Utley, Robert M. *Lone Star Justice, The First Century of the Texas Rangers*. New York: Oxford University Press, 2002.

Welch, June Rayfield. *The Texas Senator*. Dallas: GLA Press, 1978.

Winegarten, Ruthe. *Texas Women, A Pictorial History*. Austin: Eakin Press, 1985.

Winegarten, Ruthe. *Black Texas Women, 150 Years of Trial and Triumph*. Austin: University of Texas Press, 1995.

ABOUT THE AUTHOR

Kinky Friedman lives in a hundred-year-old lodge in the heart of the Hill Country with four old dogs, not counting himself.

FOR MORE INFORMATION GO TO:

kinkyfriedman.com
or
utopiarescue.com.

ABOUT THE ARTIST

When Copper Love is not busy pursuing her art, she is traveling the world massaging racehorses. She has known KF since he came back from Borneo and they're still speaking.

FOR MORE INFORMATION GO TO:

copperlove.com